The Devil's Trap

'I have come to realise that only those who have known paralysing fear, have felt the deepest abstract anxiety and been assured the perfect knowledge of complete and utter abandonment can fully understand what those poor souls went through.'

Mark Probett

The Devil's Trap

The Victims of the Cawnpore Massacre During the Indian Mutiny

James W. Bancroft

FRONTLINE
BOOKS

First published in Great Britain in 2019 by
Frontline Books
An imprint of
Pen & Sword Books Ltd
Yorkshire – Philadelphia

ISBN 978 1 52671 801 3

Printed and bound in the UK by TJ International Ltd,
Padstow, Cornwall.

Pen & Sword Books Limited incorporates the imprints of Atlas,
Archaeology, Aviation, Discovery, Family History, Fiction, History,
Maritime, Military, Military Classics, Politics, Select, Transport,
True Crime, Air World, Frontline Publishing, Leo Cooper, Remember
When, Seaforth Publishing, The Praetorian Press, Wharncliffe
Local History, Wharncliffe Transport, Wharncliffe True Crime
and White Owl.

For a complete list of Pen & Sword titles please contact

PEN & SWORD BOOKS LIMITED
47 Church Street, Barnsley, South Yorkshire, S70 2AS, England
E-mail: enquiries@pen-and-sword.co.uk
Website: www.pen-and-sword.co.uk

Or

PEN AND SWORD BOOKS
1950 Lawrence Rd, Havertown, PA 19083, USA
E-mail: Uspen-and-sword@casematepublishers.com
Website: www.penandswordbooks.com

Contents

Introduction

To anyone of sound mind this is a heartbreaking story, and it is difficult to comprehend the dreadful events described on these pages. It was inhumanity at its worst, the Devil himself could not devise a more spine-chilling scenario, and people of a sensitive disposition must not read on.

Early in June 1857 the Honourable East India Company's strategic garrison at Cawnpore (Kanpur) came under siege from rebels. The British inhabitants included many non-combatant men, as well as women and children, who became caught up in the terrible events. They spent nearly two months under profound threat that put them in fear for their lives and the likelihood of a brutal death; but they could not have imagined how dreadful that death would be. They suffered from thirst, starvation, and heatstroke from the relentless scorching sun. They were holed up in a makeshift entrenchment, riddled with disease caused by the lack of sanitary provisions and their weakened state, and their numbers were being seriously depleted from continuous bombardment by cannonballs and bullets from rebel snipers.

On being promised safe passage out of the city by boats provided by the rebel leaders, most of the men were treacherously massacred at the Sati Chaura Ghat, a landing stage on the banks of the River Ganges. The surviving women and children were imprisoned in a house known as the Bibighar, 'The House of Ladies', to await their fate. This fate came on Wednesday, 15 July 1857, when at least five men, including butchers from the local bazaar, slaughtered them with swords and cleavers in a murderous frenzy. On the following morning their naked remains were unceremoniously dragged outside and thrown down a well. At least six of these victims were still clinging on to life, including three children. The culprits of this disturbing atrocity were not of the human race they were representatives of Satan. For armed individuals to attack and take the lives of defenceless people in any way is sinking to the lowest depths of sickening cowardice.

History books record that in the mid-Victorian era there was supposedly a growing sympathy for children and an idealisation of the innocence of childhood – this was evidently not the case everywhere. The child victims did not understand the actions of the adults around them – British and Indian – which put them in a nightmare that no human of any age should have to suffer, and the heartbreak and feelings of hopelessness endured by the women who tried to protect them before they too were put out of their misery is impossible to imagine by anyone who has not suffered it. British retribution was equally merciless and repugnant, and two wrongs don't make a right.

At Cawnpore the desire to defend Indian beliefs was tarnished by the root of all evil – money. Nana Sahib, the rebel leader, was embittered towards the British because the lucrative pension that had been afforded to his late adopted father was not passed to him, and the murderers at the Bibighar are believed to have performed their sick and depraved act for the reward of one rupee for every life they took.

Much has been written about the siege of Cawnpore and the political events which caused it, but there is not much information in book form concerning the people who suffered the ordeal. Who were they, and where did they come from? They left behind parents who were deeply bereaved, with no individual grave over which to grieve them. In many cases victims' deaths devastated their families and produced numerous orphans. I have tried to present an informative selection of the type of people who were involved; although I am sure there will be some I have omitted who should have been included. In many cases this is because there was not enough information about them to justify a full biographical tribute.

For instance, one victim had worked with the engineer, Isambard Kingdom Brunel when he was at the height of his career; a member of a family of victims later became a well-known cricketer and footballer, who gained three Football Association Challenge Cup winner's medals; the brother of one of the victims, who was himself a defender of Lucknow, later played cricket for Lancashire; and another was a descendant of an Anglo–Norman West Country family. I have tried to redress this imbalance of information by consulting official documentation and establishments, studying primary sources and contacting descendants, then cross-referencing and checking the information as much as possible through some previous publications and online sites such as Ancestry.com and Forces-War-Records.co.uk.

In addition to this, I have consulted my JWB Historical Library, a project that I began four decades ago, and which is now one of the largest collections of information of its kind not in an official archive. Using this method I tried to highlight the human element of the horrific events, and provide revised information where necessary.

To try to understand opinions on both sides I have also studied documents and contacted individuals who believe the events at Cawnpore were part of India's first steps in the struggle towards eventual independence, which was finally achieved in 1947. These individuals have no misgivings concerning what happened. In some cases I organised personal meetings so that I could look through the eyes and into the souls of people who said they believed that what happened at Cawnpore was justified.

On a visit to the Sati Chaura Ghat, Sir Frederick Treves, the prominent Victorian surgeon who witnessed the hurtful sufferings of Joseph Merrick, known as the Elephant Man, wrote 'This is probably the very bitterest spot on Earth; this murderer's stare; this devil's trap; this traitor's gate. The very stones are trained and festered with hate, and until it rots, the mud-covered colonnade will be found with the sneaking shadows of cowardice.' A descendant of one of the victims who visited the city stated 'Some spirit of evil still seems to haunt the place.'

There are evil people in all walks of life, and when I was ten years old I too came face to face with some of Satan's disciples. During the summer of 1963 I was playing with some friends outside the gates of my school in Salford. The school was built at the time of the Indian Rebellion and was opened in 1859. There was a steep pathway between the school building and an ironworks, known locally as 'Polefield Brow', and beyond was a large stretch of open land known as 'Duchy Hills', which, with hindsight, I realized constituted an easy getaway. One of my friends suddenly brought my attention to a woman standing at the bottom of the path staring at us around the corner of the school, who she said had beckoned her with her finger. She was quite well-dressed, but I remember her hair was like a grotesque straw wig and she looked menacing. She turned and moved away, so I took tentative steps to the corner and looked up the path. The makeshift boundary fence of the ironworks was made of planks standing on end (known as railway sleepers), with leafy branches draping over the top. She was standing near the fence speaking to a man wearing a smart suit, but the thing that made me shudder about him were his cold penetrating eyes. All my friends came up behind me and began to make a fuss, and when a couple of adults walking by began to look over at us to see what was going on the two sinister characters seemed to realise that they had attracted too much attention, and we were relieved when they turned and walked away up the path.

I shuddered with horror when I first read the story of the Cawnpore massacres in the same way that I shuddered with dread when I realised who those two people were on seeing pictures of the Moors Murderers.

James W Bancroft, 2019

Chapter 1

The Devil's Wind

The Indian Rebellion was the most ferocious and sustained explosion of violence in the history of the British Empire. It tested Britain's colonial resources to the limit, and nearly brought about the downfall of Britain's rule in India and the loss of the jewel in the crown.

British authority in India had caused tension and unease among the population for many years prior to the rebellion. They had shown an attempt to westernise Indian traditions, which struck at the very heart of Indian life, and the people dreaded what the future had in store for them. In 1857 feelings ran particularly high and some kind of strong reaction from the population was inevitable.

Although made after the conflict, a statement by Begum Hazrat Mahal of Oudh, who rebelled against the British, contains elements that touch on the real truth of what caused the tragedy in northern India in 1857:

'That religion is true which acknowledges one God and knows no other. Where there are three gods in a religion, neither Mussulman (Muslim) or Hindus – nay, not even Jews, sun-worshippers or fire-worshippers – can believe it to be true. To eat pigs and drink wine, to bite greased cartridges and to mix pig's fat with flour and sweetmeats, to destroy Hindu and Mussulman temples on pretence of making roads, to build churches, to send clergymen into the streets and alleys to preach the Christian religion, to institute English schools and pay people a monthly stipend for learning the English sciences, while the places of worship of Hindu and Mussulman are to this day neglected – with all this how can the people believe that religion will not be interfered with? The rebellion began with religion, and for it millions of men have been killed. Let not our subjects be deceived; thousands were deprived of their religion in the north-west and thousands were hanged rather than abandon their religion.'

The governor-general of India was a king in all but name, and his remoteness from London gave him the freedom to rule almost as he pleased. He could overrule his advisers in Britain and until the growth of better communications a decade or so after the rebellion he had absolute power on the sub-continent.

Sir James Andrew Broun-Ramsay, the First Marquess Dalhousie, became governor-general of India in 1847, and in the following year he led the British forces in a second war against the Sikhs of the Punjab. The Sikhs proved to be a formidable enemy in both wars, but the victory at Gujarat on 21 February 1849 delivered the Punjab to the British. He also commanded the British in the Anglo–Burmese War of 1852.

He was an able administrator and an extremely hard-working man, and he found time to introduce many internal reforms in India, which in his mind would be a powerful force towards India's prosperity and unity. However, his administration ruled with authoritarianism, and although he seems to have been well-intentioned in his efforts to improve Indian society, some of his actions were considered to interfere with local culture and religion. It was his driving modernisation, which the Indians thought was being forced upon them, that caused unrest and suspicion among the population. Notably, he used all the means in his power to prevent the old practice of suttee, when a widow was expected to throw herself on her husband's funeral pyre, and even legitimated the re-marriage of Hindu women.

With the help of Englishmen who joined mad dogs in the noonday sun, many engineering advances were stimulated by Lord Dalhousie, who set up India's first Ministry of Public Works. With new contraptions such as R. E. Compton's road steamer, which far outclassed bullock haulage, British engineers began the construction of the metal-based east–west Grand Trunk Road in 1839, knocking down anything in its way – including mosques. In towns such as Cawnpore other new inventions such as the telegraph were not understood by the ordinary people, and the building of railways and travel in such a way upset the ideas of caste.

Under Lord Dalhousie's administration, the British implemented the policy of 'doctrine of lapse', which ensured that if a king did not have any sons for a natural heir, the kingdom would be annexed for the British Empire. Using this policy the British took over several princely states, such as Mandvi, Kolaba, Jaloun, Surat, Satara, Jhansi, Jaitpur, Sambalpur, Udaipur, Bhagat and Nagpur, and when Oudh was annexed in 1856 it caused distrust in the region, antagonised the deposed princes, and made Dalhousie extremely unpopular. In addition to this, landowners found their estates being confiscated because they had no deeds to prove their ownership, because such things were unknown in India. The 1st Earl Canning took over the office of governor-general on 28 February 1856, and it was during his administration that the lapse and annexation policy was abolished.

The Indian private soldiers, known as sepoys, considered themselves to be the essential part of British military power in India. They were said to be quite tall, the average height being about five feet eight inches. They never became completely military in their tastes and habits, but they were reasonably well paid. The usual uniform was red tunic with black trousers, which they were said to get out of as soon as they possibly could after being dismissed from duty. They were already aware that they vastly outnumbered the British soldiers, and the campaigns in Afghanistan and the Crimea had shaken their faith in British superior power. Brigadier John Nicholson CB stated 'For years I have watched the army and felt sure they only wanted their opportunity to try their strength with us.'

There had been several incidents previously that had caused near-mutinies, usually from suspicions that overzealous British officers were attempting to gradually convert them to Christianity by forcing them to violate the tenets of their own religions. On 10 July 1806, in the fort at Vellore, in southern India, sepoys of the Madras Native Infantry revolted because they were ordered to trim their beards, wear restyled turbans and give up caste-marks. The rebellion was immediately put down by soldiers of the 69th (South Lancashire) Regiment. More than 100 British soldiers were casualties and there were nearly 1,000 sepoy casualties and executions. In 1824 a sepoy regiment refused to embark for war in Burma, because travel by sea would have rendered them outcastes. Six of the ring-leaders were hanged and hundreds more condemned to fourteen years' hard labour on the public roads. Five others were later executed and their bodies hung in chains as an example to their followers.

The 1857 uprising was not national and was confined mainly to the north, from Bengal to the Punjab, and central India. The majority of support for the rebellion came from the army and recently dethroned princes, but in some areas it developed into a peasant uprising and general revolt, which seems to have been the case with Cawnpore. Within three weeks the whole of the Ganges basin was aflame with discontent.

The immediate spark that enflamed the situation occurred when the British Army introduced the new Enfield gun that replaced the old 'Brown Bess', which offered improved accuracy and rapidity of fire. The sensitivity of Indian soldiers was offended by reports that the rifles came with new issues of cartridges that had been smeared with pig and cow fat. This defiled the beliefs of both Muslims and Hindus, as the pig is forbidden to Muslims and the cow sacred to Hindus. Many regiments refused to use them, and were punished for their insubordination, causing deep resentment, and a general feeling of unrest festered among the Indian military. However, evidence suggests that there would have been a rebellion even without the bullet controversy.

Rumours of the greased cartridges were circulated at Dum Dum in January 1857, and reached Berhampur, a military station about 90 miles north of Barrackpore, which itself is about 15 miles north of Calcutta. Another rumour was circulated 'that they were to be baptised, and we hear that they are greatly alarmed in consequence. It should be explained to them that the only ceremony of the kind to which soldiers are required to submit is the baptism of fire.'

As if to further agitate unrest in the station, a letter was received at Barrackpore stating 'Bungalows here are set fire to every night,' and on 10 February an individual described simply as a Hindu apparently warned the governor:

My Lord, this is the most critical time ever reached in the administration of British India. Almost all the independent native Princes and Rajas have been so much offended at the late Annexation policy that they have begun to entertain deadly enmity to the British Empire in India. Moreover, as for the internal defences of the

Empire, the cartridge question has created a strenuous movement in some portions of the Hindu sepoys, and will spread it through all their ranks over the whole country to the great insecurity of British rule.

There were no European troops at the station, only the 19th Bengal Native Infantry, a squadron of native cavalry, and a battery of guns manned by sepoys. At a parade on 27 February 1857, the infantrymen refused to accept an issue of cartridges, which they believed were of the new kind although it turned out that this was not the case. Nevertheless, the situation was handled badly by the officer in command, Colonel Mitchell, and discipline broke down. The colonel became conciliatory when he realised that the artillery and cavalry might side with the infantry, but he reported the incident to Calcutta, and the 19th Bengal Native Infantry were marched down to Barrackpore to be disbanded.

Yet another agitating rumour circulated around Barrackpore that the 87th (Royal Irish) Fusiliers were hastily being brought back from Burma to attack the sepoys. Their actual duty was to supervise the disbandment of the 19th, but on the afternoon of 29 March a more serious incident occurred. The commander at Barrackpore was General John Hearsey of the 2nd Bengal Irregular Cavalry (Gardner's Horse), who received a report that there was trouble on the parade ground. When he and his son, also named John, arrived, a horrific sight met his eyes. A sepoy of the 34th Native Infantry named Mangal Pandey had begun causing trouble. It was suggested that he was under the influence of some kind of drug. While resisting arrest he had cut down Adjutant Baugh and the regimental sergeant-major, after which he called for his comrades to join him and die bravely for their religion and caste.

There was a group of officers standing at the corner of the parade ground, including the officer of Pandey's regiment, all apparently too shocked to take any kind of action. One of these men called out to Hearsey 'Have a care! His musket is loaded!' 'Damn his musket!' replied the general, and turning to his son he said 'If I fall, John, rush in and put him to death somehow!' As Hearsey ran towards Pandey, the sepoy raised his musket – then turned it on himself and pulled the trigger, wounding himself. The 19th was disbanded at the end of March, Mangal Pandey was tried by court martial and hanged on 8 April 1857, and the 34th Native Infantry was partially disbanded. Mangal Pandey's name lived on as it became the Indian signal for revolt, and a 'pandey' became a general derogatory term used by the British for all Indians.

Full-scale rebellion first broke out seriously at the important garrison station of Meerut, which lies 40 miles to the north-east of Delhi. On 9 May, eighty-five troopers of the 3rd Bombay Light Cavalry were brought up on the parade ground, in the presence of the whole force there, to receive the sentence of a general court-martial. Their offence was disobedience, in refusing to fire with the cartridges supplied to them, which were in reality the same as those they had been using for several months. However, a rumour had been spread among the sepoys that the British government was attempting to interfere with the caste system by introducing cartridges soaked in animal fat. They were sentenced to ten years' imprisonment with hard labour, and were marched off in chains to the local jail.

All remained quiet until the following evening of Sunday, 10 May. The main body of British troops were in their quarters some distance away, and the officers were unarmed as they attended a church parade with their families. Men of the 11th and 20th Bengal Native Infantry saw their chance and rose in mutiny. They fired on their officers, and Lieutenant-Colonel John Finnis of the 20th Bengal Native Infantry became the first European officer killed in the rebellion. They were soon joined by the 3rd Bombay Light Cavalry. The rebels stormed the jail and set it on fire to release the sepoys, and more than 1,000 prisoners were also liberated, who, with the rabble of the town, at once sided with the sepoys, and committed dreadful atrocities. The 2,200 troops in the European lines were not used to oppose the mutineers, as every European who got in their way was attacked, and a great number of officers and civil administrators, together with women and children, were barbarously treated in an orgy of murder and rape, arson, a general destruction of British property and Christian places of worship, and looting.

Some murders received particular notoriety, and one eyewitness stated:

Bungalows began to blaze round us nearer and nearer, till the frenzied mob reached that next to our own! We saw a poor lady in the veranda, a Mrs Charlotte Chambers (lately arrived). We bade the servants bring her over the low wall to us, but they were too confused to attend to me at first. The stables of that house were first burnt. We heard the shrieks of the horses. Then came the mob to the house itself, with awful shouts and curses. We heard the doors broken in, and many, many shots, and at the moment my servant said they had been to bring away Mrs Chambers, but had found her dead on the ground, cut horribly, and she on the eve of her confinement. Oh, night of horrors!

In fact, her unborn child had been ripped from her stomach by a local butcher. She was the wife of Captain R. W. Chambers, who was the adjutant of the 11th Bengal Native Infantry.

Eliza Dawson, the wife of Veterinary-Surgeon Charles John Dawson of the 3rd Bombay Light Cavalry, was recovering from smallpox. To avoid going near her and risking contagion, the mob threw burning torches at her until her clothes caught fire and burnt her to death. Veterinary Dawson and their two children were also murdered.

Louisa Sophia MacDonald, the wife of a captain in the 20th Bengal Native Infantry, who had earlier been shot by his own men, was 'barbarously murdered' while trying to make her escape with her three infants from her burning bungalow to the British lines.

The rebels soon reached Delhi. At that time there were no European troops in Delhi, and Lieutenant Edward Vibart of the 54th Native Infantry stated:

The orderly havildar of my company came running up to my bungalow to report that the regiment had received orders to march down instantly to the city, as some troopers of the 3rd Light Cavalry had that morning arrived from Meerut and were creating disturbances.

More rebel units arrived and after more horrific bloodshed they succeeded in taking over the city. A Delhi Field Force of about 6,000 men was quickly got together under the command of General, Sir Henry Barnard, which arrived to besiege the town on 6 June 1857. In defiance of British authority, and apparently against his wishes, Bahadur Shah II, a representative of the old royal line, had been proclaimed Emperor of India.

Sir Henry Lawrence, the senior administrator of the Punjab, was in command of the Lucknow garrison. He recognised 'the uneasiness pervading the native mind', and unrest among the native soldiers was becoming serious. He foresaw trouble, so he moved all the British citizens and the small garrison of about 300 British troops and 700 loyal Indian soldiers into the Residency. The Residency came under siege from rebels on 2 July. Two days later, Lawrence was killed and command was taken over by Lieutenant-Colonel John Inglis of the 32nd Light Infantry.

However, there were no new cartridges at Cawnpore until fifteen men of the 1st Madras European Fusiliers arrived two days before there was any trouble in the city.

Chapter 2

Cawnpore and the Civilian Population

The name Cawnpore is believed to have derived from Karnapur, meaning town of Karna, who was one of the heroes of the Mahabharata, an old Indian epic saga, although it has been suggested that it is half-Mohammedan and half-Hindu – Cawn or Khan meaning Lord, and pore or poor, meaning town.

Cawnpore was selected by the East Indian Company in 1775 as the main base for troops for use with the government of Oudh (now Awadh). In 1801 most of the region of Oudh was ceded to the Company. By 1857 Cawnpore had become an important trading centre and garrison town that formed the headquarters of the command engaged to guard and defend the province of Oudh.

The town certainly needed defending, as its European community grew to become the second largest in the whole of the sub-continent. Described as a 'barbarous' place, where crime was rampant, a senior officer who was stationed there in the 1840s stated 'Cawnpore was always a hateful place … famed for being the hottest hole in India, and was looked upon as being a penal colony.' Another commented 'The country is frightful, and the dust indescribable.'

Cawnpore is in the north-west of Bengal, situated 260 miles to the east of Delhi, and about 630 miles from Calcutta by land. The city lies on the south bank of the River Ganges. During the dry season the river is about 500 yards wide, and in the rainy season more than a mile across, and navigable for light craft for 1,000 miles to the sea, and 300 miles inland to the north. Mowbray Thomson stated '… the scene which the river presents is full of life and variety; at the Ghaut (Sati Chaura) or landing-place, a busy trade is constantly plying.'

A section of the East India Railway had recently been completed there, and a toll bridge constructed of boats carried the Grand Trunk Road from Allahabad over the river, which brought travellers and detachments of troops each day, all of whom halted at Cawnpore before carrying on northwards towards Lucknow, 42 miles away.

The layout of the town was similar to all stations at that time, being separated into three distinct areas. These were the native town with its main thoroughfare known as the Chouk, with narrow streets leading off it to bazaars and markets; the civil lines consisting of administrative offices such as the treasury, the church, the local jail, and the bungalows of the European inhabitants; and the military lines to the west of the main town, which were separated by a canal, and ran along the banks of the river in a semicircle shape extending for about 6 miles, containing barracks for 7,000 men. Just out of the town was Mahomed's Hotel, which became the rebel headquarters, and was about 100 yards from the Bibighar.

Numerous European and Eurasian merchants and shopkeepers, officials and workers of the East India Railway and the Post Office lived in the main town and went about their business there. The state of marriage was considered particularly special in India and most couples had many children. There were also a large number of mixed race children in the Cawnpore school. The total number of Europeans was well over 1,000 people.

Charles George Hillersdon was the magistrate and collector in the Cawnpore district. He was born on 3 February 1822, at St Mary's Parish in Barnes, now in the London borough of Richmond, the son of John Grove Hillersdon (born in 1785), and his wife, Maria (formerly Reade), who had married on 19 February 1808, at St Giles Church in Camberwell, south London. Charles was educated at the Imperial Services College at Haileybury near Hertford, from 1838 to 1840, where he was the youngest in his class, and soon afterwards he was given a posting to India. He had spent sixteen of the next thirty-five years serving the Company in India, and in 1851 he became joint-magistrate and collector of the south division at Bundelkhand in Banda, and magistrate and collector at Cawnpore in January 1857. He was 'an active and judicious man', who got on with his tasks of administration with great vigour, and even found time to act as patron of the civilian cricket team.

He married Lydia Lucy Prole (born on 20 October 1835 at Mynpooree, West Bengal) at Calcutta on 24 February 1853. She was the daughter of

Major George Newton Prole of the Bengal Army, (born in Calcutta on 8 June 1801, died in Cheltenham on 15 September 1839), and his wife, Margaret Tierney (formerly Fergusson, 1807–68), who had married in Cawnpore on 7 November 1826. The 1841 census records the family living at Park's Place in Charlton Kings near Cheltenham. There is a memorial dedicated to George Newton Prole inside Holy Trinity Church in Cheltenham, and to several other members of the Prole family.

Lydia was thirteen years younger than Charles, and together they had two children; with a third child on the way. John Derville was born at Geneva in Switzerland on 22 July 1854, and christened at St Mary's Church in Marylebone, London, on 16 November 1854. Lydia was born on 28 July 1856 in Cawnpore, and she was christened in Cawnpore on 30 August 1856.

The Hillersdons lived in a spacious bungalow at Nawabganj. Lydia was a good musician, especially on the piano and concertina. She was an admirer of the works of Felix Mendelssohn, and she was a favourite of the piano virtuoso Joseph Ascher. She was apparently 'softly spoken', and Mowbray Thomson said of her 'Mrs Hillersdon was a most accomplished lady, and by reason of her cheerfulness, amiability and piety, universally a favourite at the station.'

Other members of the family serving in Cawnpore were Charles' 39-year old brother, Major William Reade Hillersdon, and Lydia's cousin, Lieutenant William George Prole, both of whom were with the 53rd Bengal Native Infantry. Lieutenant Prole was born in Calcutta on 13 December 1835, the son of William Sandys Prole (born 1803, died at Nusseerabad in June 1846), and his wife, Harriett (formerly Dobbin, born in 1810, died at Bridgwater in Somerset in 1895). William was christened in Calcutta on 18 December 1835.

Samuel Greenway was the owner of a large indigo factory named Greenway Brothers of Cawnpore and Najafgarh until his death on 23 June 1822. Bengal was the biggest producer of indigo in the world during the nineteenth century. The plants named indigofera tinctoria were soaked in large tanks or vats of water to release their blue colour, which would float to the top to be retrieved and dried. Indian dress of sari blouse and other long draping fabrics were always brightly coloured by tradition and indigo was treasured for its rich blue colour and because it was one of the most colourfast natural dyes.

Samuel had married Rose Anne Anderson at Calcutta on 25 August 1801. They had thirteen children, and Edward Francis was running the business in 1857. Edward had been born on 18 March 1808 in Calcutta. He married Georgina Clementine, aged sixteen, on 14 December 1829 at Cawnpore. She was the daughter of Captain Austin Neame Acres. Another son called Samuel was involved in the business. Edward had a fourteen-year-old son named Thomas, and twins named Louisa Evelina and Rose Mary.

William Morris Probett was running the DAK Inland Freight Company, which was based in the Cawnpore area. William's type of work demanded a man of tough constitution and having been in the Horse Artillery he knew how to handle heavy beasts and equipment. In 1852 he was listed as running the Golden Horse DAK, which ran dhoolies and wagons throughout Bengal. He was also a horse vet and manager with the DAK Inland Transport Company.

This kind of employment with the DAK called for an energetic and resourceful man of stamina and fortitude, and the work often saw William up to 900 miles or more away from home and family, sometimes down near Calcutta long before the East India Railway tracks had been laid. The teams of four horses or bullocks per carriage were always being driven hard on India's Main Trunk Road, and sometimes the strong beasts reared up and had to be brought back under control by the driver. When a carriage came to a fordable river, the driver and coolies had to pull the carriages across, which could take up to two hours. The long wearisome journey was broken only by the relief of government-built DAK bungalows every 10 to 15 miles apart. The DAK bungalow was an inn or rest-house, one-storeyed, and often built on a knoll, with scant furniture and even scantier provisions.

William had been born at Wollaton in Nottingham, and was baptised at All Saints Church in Leamington Priors, Warwickshire, on 27 October 1813. He was the son of Stephen Probett and his wife Ann (formerly Dixon), and he had two brothers and two sisters. He found his work as a general labourer too tedious, so he lied about his age, and on 27 July

1829 at Westminster he became a gunner with the 1st Troop, 3rd Brigade, Bengal Horse Artillery, in the East India Company's army. He sailed to India aboard the steam ship *Dunera* with the regiment, and arrived in Calcutta on 3 May 1830. He was described as being 5ft 6in tall, with dark hair and dark eyes, with a long face and a fresh complexion. He purchased his discharge from military service on 12 June 1844.

His father died in 1838, and on 8 September of the same year he married Amy Gatland Izzard, who was just thirteen years old and was attended by her parents, at St John's Soldiers' Chapel within the Cawnpore cantonment, and they had several children, of whom four are known. Stephen John was born on 13 December 1842, and died on 25 March 1846; William Gearge was born on 5 May 1845, and died on 25 November 1849; Charles Thomas was born on 7 May 1845, and survived the rebellion; and Amy Ruth was born on 5 August 1849. Unfortunately, Amy Gatland died on 30 March 1852.

On 5 July 1852, William married a young girl named Ellen Walsh at St John's Church. Together they had six children, Emma, Louise, Nellie and John, two of them at least being twins, and the last two were William Stephen, born on 16 August 1855, and Kate Ann Margaret, born on 18 October 1856. They were all present at Cawnpore, along with Amy Ruth. Charles Thomas was a pupil at the La Martiniere School in Lucknow. Ellen's sister, Catherine, was married to William Walsh (railway department?). They too had six children, and Ellen's two young brothers, John William and Henry, were also pupils at the La Martiniere School.

Katherine Jemima 'Kate' Lindsay and her family lived in Cawnpore. She was born in Dundee in about 1804. Her husband, George, had been a senior civil servant in Benares and a judge in Delhi. They had four children. Caroline Ann was born in Dundee on 17 February 1834, and the other three children were born in India; Alice on 8 January 1837, George on 17 December 1838, and Frances Davidson, known as Fanny, on 5 December 1841.

George became an ensign in the 1st Bengal Native Infantry in 1856, and Kate's sister, Lillias 'Lily' Don, was married to Major William Lindsay of the 10th Bengal Native Infantry (probably her husband's brother), who was stationed at Benares. He was born in 1810, the son of William M Lindsay, a Dundee grain merchant. There is still a William M. Lindsay grain merchants in Scotland, which celebrated its 150th anniversary in 2014. William joined the service in 1826, and became a major in 1854. They had three children.

As he was only in his late forties, ill health had possibly caused George Lindsay to retire. He lived at Blackheath in Kent, and died in the United States in October 1849. A family vault at St Luke's Church in Charlton near Woolwich includes the body of George Lindsay, Bengal Civil Service, who died on 25 October 1849, aged forty-nine. It is not certain if Kate and the family came home with George or just for his funeral, but the 1851 census states that they lived at 32 Union Street (now the Union Street car park), at St Margaret's Parish in Rochester. Kate was described as a forty-seven-year-old widow, whose occupation was given as 'fund holder'.

Rochester has an intriguing connection with Charles Dickens, who had a close association with the town all his life; including at the time when the Lindsay family lived there. He was originally from Chatham, but he came to know Rochester as a child, and his writings include a great number of local associations. He settled at Gad's Hill Place on the Rochester to Gravesend road in March 1856, where he was visited by several prominent writers of the day, including a five-week stay in 1857 by the famous Danish children's author, Hans Christian Andersen, whose fairy stories would have been familiar to the Lindsay family and other young people of Cawnpore.

Kate had enjoyed her life in India, going to dinner parties, concerts, and even excursions to the races, and she longed to go back, so after the death of her husband she began to prepare to do so. Encouraging her son George to follow in his father's footsteps and forge a career with the East India Company, he attempted to enrol at the Company's college at Haileybury, but he failed the entrance examination. However, he managed to get a place at the military school at Addiscombe. On his passing out, Kate took Fanny out of school and against the wishes of her family, including Caroline and Alice, they set off back to the sub-continent in July 1856, and arrived there in October.

Caroline wrote many letters home to her aunt, Kate's sister, Mary Jane, who was married to the Reverend William Henry Drage, vicar of

St Margaret's Church in Rochester, and in November 1856, she told of a meeting with her Lindsay cousins at Barrackpore in Calcutta. One of these was William Lindsay, who would find fame in the field of sport. They arrived in Benares on 11 November 1856, after a tiring journey, for what would have been an emotional reunion, and then they all set off for Cawnpore.

For some reason Caroline had great reservations about travelling up to Cawnpore. Perhaps she had had enough of the rough journeys? However, while in Benares they visited Lieutenant-Colonel Ramsey, whose wife was a cousin of Caroline's. On learning the news of the fate of the Lindsay family, he later noted that:

> they had gone to Cawnpore in high spirits, except this poor girl, who cried bitterly, and asked to be left with us; which we would gladly have consented to. From some presentiment she appeared afraid to go up country, but her mother would not hear of her remaining. At that time there was not even a shadow apparent of all that was to happen.

Susanna 'Susan' Kennedy was born in India in 1808, probably in Cawnpore because most of her siblings were born in the town. She was the oldest in the family of eleven daughters and four sons of General James Kennedy (1778–1859) of the 5th Bengal Light Cavalry, and his wife Anna (formerly Don, 1787–1884). General Kennedy was descended from the Scottish Earls of Cassilis. The 5th Cavalry was a unit that served in the occupation of Kabul in 1841, and part of the regiment acted as the rearguard during the disastrous retreat from Kabul, when it was wiped out. The remainder of the regiment took part in the defence of Jellalabad, in the Kabul campaign of 1842, and in both Anglo–Sikh Wars of 1845-46 and 1848-49.

Susan was just sixteen years old when she married the dashing Lieutenant Edward McLeod Blair (born 13 May 1803) of her father's regiment, on 2 August 1824, in Muttra (now Mathura) in the Agra district. Lieutenant Blair was the son of Major-General, Sir Robert Blair KCB, and his wife, Herculina Elizabeth (formerly Durham, 1772–1822). Sir Robert was born at Fife in Scotland in 1754, and died in Bath on 11 February 1837.

Their eight children were all born in India. Edward Robert was born on 25 May 1825 at Keitah in West Bengal. However, he died aged eleven on 6 December 1836 in Burma (Myanmar); Eliza was born on 4 October 1826 at Kylat in West Bengal; James was born on 27 January 1828 at Nimach in Rajasthan; Charlotte was born on 11 September 1831 at Karnaul in the Punjab; Isabella was born in 1834 in India; Robert was born on 1 August 1835 at Cawnpore; Charles Renny was born on 14 February 1837 in Cawnpore; and Susan junior was born on 18 July 1840 at Kunool. The girls were said to be 'Remarkable for their refined beauty, which they inherited from their mother.'

After visiting his then pregnant wife and family in Cawnpore and Benares, Lieutenant Blair went on active service in Afghanistan in 1840. During the retreat from Kabul on 12 January 1842, he was reported as lost in action at the difficult and dangerous Jagdalak Mountain Pass (now the Lataband Pass). However, no official reports of his death were received by his family, and Susan lived in hope that he was still alive somewhere in captivity.

Susan brought her family home from India to live in her husband's former home in the city of Bath, famous for its Roman spa. The houses are built of the light-coloured local Bath stone, as was their home at 19 Macauley Buildings at Lyncombe and Widcombe Hill (which still exists). Susan is described as an accountant, and as devout Christians they worshipped at the local St Matthew's Church. They also had a niece named Alice Waterfield, and three servants living at the house. However, Susan probably received her husband's Kabul Medal, which would have often reminded her of him. She could not settle because of her desire to learn of his true fate, and as many of her family had remained in India she, Isabella and Susan left the beauty of Bath for the sub-continent. Captain Mowbray Thomson described her as an 'estimable lady'.

They went to live with her sister, Charlotte, who was married to Doctor Arthur Wellesley Robert Newenham, who had been the resident surgeon at the Indore Charitable Hospital, supervising ten Malwa dispensaries, before becoming attached to the 1st Bengal Native Infantry. Doctor Newenham was the son of an official of the Excise Department, and had been born in Dublin on 12 August 1812, graduated at Heidelberg University, and had been on active medical duties in the Sutlej campaign.

The trip would also give Susan the chance to visit her parents at Benares. Her sister had married Lieutenant-Colonel William Alexander, also of the 5th Bengal Light Cavalry, and they had eight children; one of them being Augustus Hay, who was stationed at Cawnpore with the 68th Bengal Native Infantry. Charlotte married her cousin, Captain (later Major-General) William Ruxton Eneas Alexander of the 53rd Bengal Native Infantry, at the Indian Office in Benares, on 11 September 1850. Captain Alexander was a veteran of the Second Anglo–Sikh War who had fought at Gujarat.

Susan's daughter, Charlotte, was with her husband, Captain Alexander, stationed at Oorai, a detached command in the district situated across the River Jumna about 80 miles from Cawnpore. When the Indian Rebellion broke out, he and his fellow officer, Lieutenant Tomkinson, were approached by the native NCOs of their regiment and were informed that they had each taken over command of their company, but that they did not intend to harm their old friends. They provided Captain Alexander and Charlotte with a camel and recommended that they make their way to Agra as best they could, as they could not be responsible for their safety if they remained. After showing their disapproval of the situation, they set off, and after many perils they finally reached the comparative safety of the fort at Agra. Lieutenant Tomkinson made his way to Gwalior, and when that contingent mutinied he was killed.

Amelia Anne 'Amy' Horne was born on 9 January 1839 in Calcutta. She was the daughter of Captain Frederick William Horne (born in 1804), who was in the employ of the East India Company, and his wife, Emma Elizabeth (formerly Smith), who was born in 1838, the daughter of John Smith of Purneah, and Marie Anne (formerly Flouest). They were both Eurasian, and prominent indigo trading families.

Captain Horne died in 1840, and Emma married John Hampden Cook (born in 1826). In February 1857, John began working as an agent for a businessman in Lucknow named John R. Brandon, who owned the North-Western Dawk Company, and they lived near a very busy and noisy iron bridge. Described as a 'pretty and vivacious girl' and a 'gifted pianist', Amy detested Lucknow, with its strange houses and dirty narrow streets, and considered the people to be 'the most indecent and abusive set ….'

Soon after a gang of local thugs surrounded her while she was out walking one evening, and threw a garland around her neck, the family moved to Cawnpore in April 1857. John Brandon had already moved most of his interests to Cawnpore, such as a store, a press, and a railway contracting company; his main business rivals being the Greenway Brothers.

Emma and John had six more children. Robert Hampden (born in 1847); Florence Trevor (born in 1849); William Thomas Hampden (born in 1851); Ethel Trevor (born in 1852); Herbert Hampden (born in 1853); and Mary Trevor (born in 1855). All nine members of the family were at Cawnpore when the rebellion broke out.

Isabel Georgina White was born at East Reach, Taunton St James in Somerset, and she was baptised on 1 July 1829, the oldest surviving daughter in the large family of John Eales White, who ran the East Reach Brewery of Taunton St James, and his wife, Sophia. The brewery was taken over by his son, Frederick, as A. and F. White when her father died in 1855.

Isabel was a friend of Louisa Parsons Chalwin, who was married to Edward George Chalwin, a veterinary surgeon of the 2nd Bengal Light Cavalry. Soon after John White died, Louisa was on a trip to England when she persuaded Isabel to return to Cawnpore with her, with the intention of finding her a suitor among the young men in the town. Louisa was on reasonably good terms with the Nana Sahib, who she referred to as the 'Gentleman of Bithur', after he had apparently lent her a piano while hers was being repaired. Louisa considered the society in Cawnpore to be 'very pleasant and sociable', and she spent her time on the instrument singing duets at the various parties she organised for her many guests, among them being the eligible bachelors she attempted to match-make with Isabel. She herself was suffering from loss of hair, which she tried to remedy by rubbing an onion on her scalp.

It is not certain why Eliza Guthrie was at Cawnpore, with her daughter, Catherine, unless Captain Guthrie was stationed there on the invalid station. She had been born Eliza Griffiths, and had married Captain Charles Guthrie of the 46th (South Devonshire) Regiment, at Serampore in 1832; and Catherine was born to them in India. Charles went on active service in the First Anglo–Burmese War of 1824–26, where he was seriously wounded in the leg. It would seem that his leg injury deteriorated over the years as he died in May 1843, on his way from Dinapur (Danapur) to Calcutta to have the limb amputated.

In his autobiography Thomas Guthrie DD, Charles' brother, who was a well-known preacher and philanthropist, stated 'As I may not have occasion to speak of my brother and schoolfellow again, I may mention that he afterwards became a captain in the Indian Army, and died on the banks of the Ganges in consequence of injuries suffered years before in the first Burmese War; leaving a widow, who, with her daughter, was among the massacred at Cawnpore.'

John Robert Mackillop was born at Calcutta on 1 November 1826. He was the third son of seven children to George Mackillop, originally from Stirlingshire, who was an agent for Cruttenden and Mackillop, a highly successful family of tea merchants based in Calcutta, which he ran with his brother, James. His mother was Jean Eleanor (formerly Hutton, 1800–59). They had married at St John's Church in Calcutta.

It was traditional for families to return to the UK for their children's education, and on doing so they lived at 11 Ainslie Place in Edinburgh. John was educated at Bishopwearmouth in Sunderland, and Haileybury College from 1844 to 1846. The family moved to Tasmania, where they owned businesses and land, but they returned to England in about 1846, and lived in a town house at 26 Grosvenor Place in Bath.

John arrived in India in 1847 to join the Bengal Civil Service. He was joint magistrate at Cawnpore, and his brother, Charles William, was also in the Bengal Civil Service.

Mary Anne Darby had a newborn infant with her. She was the wife of Assistant-Surgeon Edmund Darby, who was serving with the 10th Oudh Irregular Cavalry at Lucknow. She was born in Westminster, London, in 1838, the fourth child of twelve to John Jackson (born on 28 April 1799, died 2 June 1869), and his second wife, Honoria Anne Maria (formerly Daniell) who died on 25 May 1869, just a week before her husband. Mr Jackson had two children from a previous marriage. Doctor Darby was fatally wounded by a shell at Lucknow on 27 October 1857.

Chaplain Edward Theophilus Russell Moncrieff of the Ecclesiastical Department lived in a villa on the banks of the Ganges, not far from his place of worship at Christ Church in one direction and the Sati Chaura Ghat in the other. In addition to his duties at Christ Church he was also a director of the Cawnpore Free School. Described as 'muscular', he was married with a child.

The Lindsay family seemed to have no patience with him, describing him as 'clumsy' and 'vulgar', stating that his 'plain-speaking' sermons were 'harsh'. He was in the habit of putting other duties first, and to Lilly Lindsay's consternation he sometimes forgot to open the church on important Christian occasions.

However, Captain Thomson said of him 'Mr Moncrieff was held in high estimation by the garrison before the mutiny, on account of the zealous manner in which he discharged the duties of his sacred office, but his self-denial and consistency in the thickest of our perils made him yet more greatly beloved by us all.'

He was born on 27 May 1824, at Belfast in Ireland, the son of Alexander Moncrieff (1795–1864), who was an accountant, and his wife Jane (formerly Luttrell, 1798–1892). He had served as a protestant missionary in Hong Kong, and was living at Streatham in London when he married Caroline Bird Bramah at the parish chapel in St Pancras, London, on 26 September 1854. Caroline had been born on 1 September 1826, at Norwood in Surrey, the daughter of Edward Bramah, an engineer who was described on the marriage certificate as a gentleman. Emily Catherine Bird was born to them in Cawnpore on 14 July 1856.

Among the workers at the East India Railway were the team of engineers. Alfred Charles Heberden had once worked on the railways being constructed by the great man himself, Isambard Kingdom Brunel. Alfred was born in 1827 at the vicarage of St Nicolas Church in Bookham Street, Great Bookham, near Leatherhead in Surrey, the son of the Reverend William Heberden, vicar of St Nicolas Church, and his wife, Elvina Rainier (formerly Underwood), a doctor's daughter from London. He was baptised on 6 January 1828.

William Digges La Touche was the second son of the Reverend Thomas Digges La Touche (1799–1853), from the village of Killenaule in

County Tipperary, Ireland. The Reverend La Touch was an inventor who provided eight engineering items for the Great Exhibition of 1851. William had an older brother named Henry Christopher (1839–95), who was also a civil engineer in India.

Among the other engineers was Robert Hanna, the son of a barrister; J. C. Bayne, who had his wife and a son named Phillip with him; and A. M. M. Miller.

Chapter 3

Military Personnel in the Garrison

The Commander

In charge of the garrison at Cawnpore was Major-General, Sir Hugh Massy Wheeler. He had served in India since 1805, commanding troops in Afghanistan and the Punjab, but no amount of experience in the sub-continent could possibly prepare him for what he was about to face.

Also at Cawnpore with him were his wife, Frances Matilda, his eldest son, Godfrey Richard, who was serving as a lieutenant with the 1st Bengal Native Infantry; his eldest daughter Eliza Matilda; and a younger daughter named Margaret Frances, who was also known as Ulrica.

Hugh was born in Ballywire, County Limerick, Ireland, on 30 June 1789, the younger of two sons of Captain Hugh Wheeler, who was in the service of the East India Company, and his wife, Margaret, the eldest daughter of the 1st Baron Massy of Duntrileague, and Rebecca Delap. His mother died in 1838 and his father remarried. He was educated at Richmond in Surrey, and at Bath Grammar School.

His military career began in April 1805, when he received a commission as lieutenant in the 24th Bengal Native Infantry, being promoted captain on 1 January 1818. He transferred to the 48th Bengal Native Infantry in 1824, and was further promoted to major in 1829, and lieutenant-colonel on 27 June 1835. Colonel Wheeler led the 48th Native Infantry during the First Anglo–Afghan War of 1838–39, taking part in the capture of Ghazni on 23 July 1839, and at Kabul. He returned to India in December 1840, and for his service he was made a Companion of the Order of the Bath (CB), and awarded the Order of the Durrani Empire (2nd Class).

In 1810 Frances Matilda had married Lieutenant-Colonel Thomas Samuel Oliver of the 5th Bengal Native Infantry, who was killed in action in 1841 during the First Anglo–Afghan War. Frances was the daughter of Lieutenant-Colonel Frederick Carleton Marsden (1803–1889), who was an officer in the East India Company Army, and an Indian woman. Her uncle was the linguist William Marsden. She had two children: Osman Marsden (born in 1810) and Thomas Oliver (born in 1811), while Colonel Wheeler had a son named Francis (or Frank) James (1816–41) from a previous relationship, who was killed in 1841 during the same campaign.

Hugh and Frances had nine children, seven of them being born before their marriage in Aligarh on 6 March 1842, and two afterwards. All the sons except Francis John joined the Bengal Army or the British Indian Army, with four of them (George, Frederick, Patrick and Robert) attaining the rank of general. George married his cousin, Margaret Alicia Massy, and their son, George Godfrey Massy Wheeler, was awarded the Victoria Cross in Mesopotamia in 1915 while serving as a major with the Hariana Lancers.

Godfrey Richard was born on 28 November 1826, and Eliza Matilda was born on 4 July 1831. Margaret Frances was born in Cawnpore on 12 August 1837, and baptised on 6 March 1842 in Aligarh, on the same day her parents were married.

During the First Anglo–Sikh War, Colonel Wheeler commanded the 1st Infantry Brigade in the Army of the Sutlej, composed of his own unit and the 50th (Queen's Own) Regiment. He was severely wounded at the battle of Mudki on 18 December 1845, but recovered in time to take part in the battle of Aliwal on 28 January 1846. The Commanding Officer, Sir Harry Smith, stated 'In Brigadier Wheeler, my second in command, I had a support I could rely on with every confidence, and most gallantly did he head his brigade.' For his services in this campaign he was made Aide-de-Camp to Queen Victoria, with the rank of colonel in the army from 3 April 1846. On 29 April 1846 he was appointed to the command of the Jalandhar Doab.

During the Second Anglo-Sikh War of 1848–49, his leadership of the Army of the Punjab in several battles gained him the congratulations of Lord Gough, who ascribed the success to 'his soldier-like and judicious arrangements', and the praise of the governor-general, who stated 'Brigadier-General Wheeler CB, has executed the several duties which have been committed to him with great skill and success, and the governor-general has been happy in being able to convey to him his thanks thus publicly.'

In April 1849, he received the thanks of both the House of Commons and the House of Lords. On 16 August 1850, he was appointed a Knight Commander of the Order of the Bath; and he was promoted to major-general in June 1854. He resumed the command of the Jalandhar Doab, and after returning to Ireland on furlough in 1853–55, on 30 June 1856 he was appointed commander of the Cawnpore Division.

32nd (Cornwall) Light Infantry

The 32nd Light Infantry was raised in 1702 by Colonel Edward Fox to fight as a unit of Marines in the War of the Spanish Succession. After being disbanded in 1713 it was re-raised in the following year. It became the 32nd (Cornwall) Light Infantry in 1782. It served at various times in Ireland, in the War of the Austrian Succession and gained several battle honours during the Napoleonic Wars, including Waterloo, in Canada, and during the Second Anglo–Sikh War of 1848–49.

Described as 'a tall, fair, vigorous Irishman, with pale-blue eyes', Captain John Moore was the third son of Captain George Moore, a former paymaster with the 32nd Light Infantry. John followed in his father's footsteps and was commissioned as ensign in the 32nd Light Infantry on 1 November 1842. He left Ireland bound for India in 1846, being promoted to lieutenant on 3 April that year. The regiment moved to Meerut in 1847. He was on active service in the Punjab during the Second Anglo–Sikh War, being present at the siege and surrender of the fort at Mooltan in 1848 and the surrender of Cheniote. He was also present for the final battle of the campaign at Gujarat, on 21 February 1849, when 25,000 British troops, under Lord Gough, defeated the main Sikh army about 60,000 strong, and brought the campaign against the Sikhs to a close. It was the first battle in which surgeons used anaesthetics in the field to carry out amputations. In 1852 he served with the regiment under Colin Campbell during the Yusufzai Expedition in the Swat Valley, North-West Frontier.

He purchased his captaincy in 1851, and in 1855 he received two years' leave of absence and returned to Ireland, but on hearing of the war with Russia in the Crimea he volunteered for active service in the east and became major-commandant in the Turkish Contingent. For his service he received the Turkish Order of the Medjidie. He returned to India in January 1857.

His wife, Caroline Edith, was with him at Cawnpore. She was the youngest daughter of Captain John Daniell, formerly of the 17th Lancers, who lived at Bellevue in County Meath, Ireland, and died on 15 May 1840.

Captain Thomson stated 'Captain Moore, who was the life and soul of our defence, was a tall, fair man, with light-blue eyes, and I believe, an Irishman by birth.' He was described as 'one of the finest field soldiers who ever served England', and 'one of the most disgracefully ignored by historians'.

In 1854, the 32nd Regiment marched from Peshawar: 'The worst station in India for everything', to Kasauli, near Simla, in the Himalayan foothills, where it remained until October 1856, when it was ordered to Lucknow. Cawnpore was reached en route in December and a depot was established consisting of Captain Moore, Lieutenant Frederick Wainwright and Ensign Evelyn Charles Hill, their families, some eighty-five non-commissioned officers and men, about fifty women, and sixty children, about a third of them being orphans.

The main body of the regiment then proceeded 40 miles up the road to Lucknow, where it was destined to provide the backbone of the Residency's defence a few months later. Thus the month of May 1857 found Captain Moore commanding the regiment's 'invalids' at Cawnpore. He fell from his horse at some time prior to the outbreak and he was nursing a broken collarbone in a sling.

Among the men of the 32nd was Sergeant William Magwood. Although William was only 4ft 10in tall and aged just fourteen, he enlisted as a boy soldier into the 70th (Surrey) Regiment, in London on 15 November 1836, as 1083 Private Magwood. He was appointed private on 15 March 1837, and until 14 January 1849 he was posted variously at Malta, the West Indies, Canada, and Ireland. He landed in India on 19 June 1849, and served with the unit at the home of the Dum Dum Arsenal, the British Royal Artillery armoury in Calcutta, and at Cawnpore, until 30 November 1851.

He transferred to the 32nd Regiment as 3540 Private Magwood, being promoted to corporal on 30 October 1853, and sergeant on 12 November

1854. He arrived back in Cawnpore in December 1856, with his wife, Eliza, and their five children: Martha, born in 1843, Ann Jane, born in 1846, John, born in 1850, Martha, born in 1852, and William, born in 1855.

Private John Bannister was born at Sedgley near Dudley in the West Midlands in 1822, and worked as a coker before enlisting in the 9th (Norfolk) Regiment in April 1841.

He arrived in India in 1842, from where he wrote many letters home to his mother that make grim reading. One of his first letters refers to the 'great slaughter of all the 44th Regiment and a great many of the 9th being killed at Kabul', in addition to reporting on depleted ranks as a result of illness and disease; he was himself admitted to hospital on several occasions, and he quickly began to regret his choice of career: 'There is no chance of me enlisting again and I have had a belly full of soldiering.'

He saw active service against the Sikhs in the Sutlej Campaign of 1845–46, being present at Moodkee, Ferozeshuhur – where he was wounded – and Sobraon, for which he received the Sutlej Medal with Moodkee and Ferozeshuhur clasps. He transferred to the 32nd Light Infantry, where he joined an unusually literate band of comrades in Corporal John Ryder, Private Henry Metcalfe and Private Robert Waterfield, who all wrote memoirs of their service with the 32nd Light Infantry in India at the same time as Private Bannister.

In March 1848, Bannister wrote 'The least crime which you may commit is punishable with a severity that is the way a poor soldier gets for fighting for his country.'

Discipline was indeed of a harsh nature, Bannister citing the story of a young artilleryman who was shot by firing squad for striking an assistant-surgeon. He was too ill to walk and the firing party failed to kill him, so a provost finished him off with a pistol shot that 'scattered the poor fellow's brain upon the plain'.

Private Bannister was next on active service against the Sikhs in the Punjab campaign, being present at the siege of Multan, and at the battle of Gujarat; for which he received the Punjab Medal with Multan and Gujarat clasps. He stated in a letter home in May 1849 'The campaign has been a very hard one but, the pride of the world we have now taken for our country the Punjab and the five rivers. The British flag is flying over Mooltan.'

In 1852, Bannister saw active service in the punitive expedition against the tribes of the Swat Valley, where he suffered a foot injury and was admitted to hospital for some months. He received the Indian General Service Medal and clasp for the campaign.

Private Bannister remained in India, and his last surviving letter home was written from Kasauli in June 1854, by which time his contempt for soldiering was patently clear, even before the suffering he endured at Cawnpore. His words of trying to persuade his brother not to allow his nephew to pursue a military career were to prove prophetic: 'Please tell my brother to take care of young John Bannister and never let him enlist for a soldier. If he does he will only repent once – and that will be all the days of his life.'

84th (York and Lancaster) Regiment

On returning from India in 1819, the 84th Regiment absorbed its 2nd Battalion, and in 1827 the unit went to Jamaica to help to quell slave riots. Having returned home in 1839, the 84th Regiment were deployed to Burma three years later, and then back to India in 1845. The main units of the regiment were stationed at Madras until they received orders to sail to Rangoon, where they stayed for nearly four years. On the outbreak of the Rebellion they received orders for active service in India and sailed to Calcutta, arriving at Dum Dum in April 1857. They moved on to Barrackpore, where they witnessed the execution of Mangal Pandey.

As they waited for more troops to arrive to form a powerful moveable column, urgent requests from the civil authorities in the north-west provinces prompted the military in Allahabad to send E and G Companies of the regiment on ahead up country; they left daily in batches of about twenty at a time. They consisted of Lieutenant David O'Brien's E Company, and Lieutenant Saunders' G Company, together with Ensign McGrath, five sergeants, five corporals, two drummers and eighty-eight privates, a total of 103 men. They arrived at Cawnpore on about 3 June, where they were stationed in the old hospital.

Frederick John Gothleipe Saunders was born at Glanmire in County Cork, Ireland, on 5 April 1826. He was the fifth son of Colonel Richard Saunders of the 60th Rifles. His brother, Herbert Frederick, who had been born at Cork on 19 June 1819, was appointed captain with the 84th Regiment on 18 April 1851.

Frederick was commissioned as ensign in the 56th (West Essex) Regiment, on 29 December 1846, and exchanged into the 84th (York and Lancaster) Regiment on 2 March 1847.

After marrying Sarah (formerly Herbert) at St John's Church in Paddington, in April 1847, he sailed to India to join his regiment on 19 August of the same year, and he was promoted lieutenant without purchase on 13 July 1850. It seems that his wife went with him on his travels because some time later they had a son named Frederick Herbert, who was with them at Cawnpore.

He had a great desire for active service, and learning that Britain had declared war on Russia and the War Office had issued incentives for the formation of a Turkish Contingent for service in the Crimea, he left India on 8 May 1854 for service with the new unit under General Robert Vivian, which served in the defence of Kerch. For his service he was awarded the Turkish Crimea Medal.

He returned to Madras on 28 December 1856, where he offered his services to take part in the Persian expedition in any capacity, but he was not employed and returned to join his regiment in Rangoon.

Thomas Mallinson was born at Huddersfield, and left his job as a labourer to enlist into the 84th Regiment on 27 January 1855. He was one of the 100 or so members of the unit's E and G companies despatched up country from Dum Dum between 19 and 24 May 1857, to bolster the troops at Cawnpore.

Private Murphy was aged eighteen when he enlisted at Cork in June 1853, and entered the 84th Regiment at Chatham. He joined the unit while it was stationed at Madras, and went with it to Rangoon before it was ordered to India.

1st Madras (European) Fusiliers

The East India Company's army included regiments of European troops as well as the native regiments, such as the 1st Madras (European) Fusiliers. They were established in 1742 by Major Stringer Lawrence, who was a friend of Robert Clive, and came to be known as 'the Father of the Indian Army'. The unit became known as 'Neil's Blue Caps' because of their striking blue forage cap covers. They had taken part in the Third Maratha War of 1817–19, gaining the battle honour *Kirkee*; the First Anglo–Burmese War of 1824–26, gaining the battle honour *Ava*; the Second Anglo–Sikh War of 1848–49, gaining the battle honours *Multan, Gujarat* and *Punjab*; and the Second Anglo–Burmese War of 1852–53, gaining the battle honour *Pegu*. Many men had gained the Indian General Service Medal. They were the only unit fully equipped with the new Enfield rifles at the outbreak of unrest. They were involved in much of the early fighting as part of the Allahabad moveable column. A small party of fifteen men of the unit force-marched from Allahabad and arrived at Cawnpore two days before the outbreak, led by Lieutenant George Glanville of the 2nd Bengal (European) Fusiliers. This brought the number of European combatants to about 200.

George Julius Glanville was born at Sconer St Germans in Cornwall on 3 October 1832, of the Anglo–Norman House of Glanville and an old Devon political family. He was the third son and fourth child in the family of seven to Francis Glanville (born St Germans in 1797, died Alderbury in Wiltshire in 1881), formerly of the Grenadier Guards and 19th Lancers, and JP DL for Devon and Cornwall, and his wife Annabel (1796–1871), who was born in London, the daughter of the right honourable Reginald Pole-Carew of East Antony in Cornwall. They married in 1821, and the family home was Catchfrench Manor at St Germans, which has gardens designed by Humphry Repton. The house and gardens are grade II listed for their special architectural and historic interest.

The 1851 census shows Francis Glanville living at Derriford House, Egg Buckland, with his wife, and three children: Jemima, aged twenty-seven; George Julius, nineteen; and Harriot, fourteen.

George was educated at Bedford Grammar School, and had entered the 2nd Bengal European Fusiliers in 1851. After returning home from India on sick leave in 1854, he joined the Turkish Contingent for service in the Crimean War. He returned to India in May 1857, and found on landing at Calcutta that the Indian rebellion had broken out. He immediately volunteered to lead the small body of the 1st Madras European Fusiliers to Cawnpore, which he reached by forced marches two days before the outbreak.

Bengal Engineers

Lieutenant Swynfen Charles Jervis was born at Neemuch in West Bengal, in 1830, the oldest child of six sons and three daughters of Colonel William Jervis of the Bengal Army (born at Mitcham in Surrey on 28 March 1806 – died at Chatkyll in Sydenham, Kent, on 6 June 1891), and his wife, Mary Amelia, daughter of Captain Hugh Dobbie RN, who lived in the Elizabethan manor house of Saling Hall near Braintree in Essex. Swynfen was a direct paternal descendant from John Jervis and Mary Swynfen of Darlaston near Stone in Staffordshire, the grandparents of John Jervis, who was created Earl St Vincent in 1797. Colonel Jervis and Mary Amelia were divorced in 1844. She became Mrs Henry Vansittart, who served in the Bengal Civil Service from 1837 to 1871. She left some diaries that contain notes on her family and personal life from 1842 to 1858, including her experiences of the Indian mutiny at Agra.

Swynfen was educated at the East India Company's Military Seminary at Addiscombe near Croydon from 1847 to 1849, at the same time as Burnett Ashburner and St George Ashe of the Bengal Field Artillery. At Addiscombe the engineer cadets had to pass examinations in 'logarithms, practical geometry, plane trigonometry, the use of chain box, sextant and theodolite'. After fourteen months of training each was required to prepare 'a well-finished plan of a system of fortification drawn by himself.' At the time of the outbreak of the rebellion he was chief engineer at Cawnpore, and his younger brother, William, was an officer with the 1st Bengal European Fusiliers taking part in operations around Delhi.

Bengal Field Artillery

Burnett Ashburner's family originated from Lancashire in England. However, he was born at a homestead named Sillwood, in Carrick near

Longford, west of Launceston in Van Diemen's Land (Tasmania), on 9 July 1829. He was the sixth son in the family of twelve children to a highly respected administrator named William Page Ashburner of Sillwood (born in Bombay on 28 December 1791, died in Brighton on 30 March 1862), and Hester Maria (born 17 March 1798, died 4 March 1838 at Sillwood), the daughter of George Elliot of Blackheath in Kent. His father was a partner in the Bombay merchants firm of Forbes and Company, who became the Mayor of Bombay in 1823. He eventually took his family to Van Diemen's Land, where he was a member of the Legislative Council from 1838 to 1844 (Van Diemen's Land was renamed Tasmania in 1856).

When his mother died, Burnett and his family returned to England, where his father married Anne, the daughter of Daniel and Elizabeth Beale of Fitzroy Square in London, and they had a son named Francis James. In 1847, he was a classmate of St George Ashe and Swynfen Jervis at Addiscombe, but he was forced to drop out in 1848 because of illness. However, he was a descendant of John Forbes, a director of the East India Company, and several of his brothers were already in the Bombay Army, including William, who had served under Napier in Scinde and in Persia, and was serving in the rebellion as a captain with the 3rd Bombay Light Cavalry. Therefore it was probably Burnett's pedigree that was instrumental in why he managed to gain a commission with the Bengal Field Artillery. When hostilities began Lieutenant Ashburner was on his way to Ferozepore. He halted at Allahabad and offered his services as an artillery officer for Cawnpore.

Lieutenant St George Ashe was born at Sitapur in India on 8 July 1830, and baptised at Ghazipore on 14 October of that year. He was the son of Major Benjamin Ashe (born in Calcutta in 1792, died in Germany in 1868) who commanded the 62nd Bengal Native Infantry, and who had been wounded while serving in Burma, and his wife Harriett (formerly Hopper, born in 1804 in Dublin, died in 1882 in London). They had married in Cawnpore on 9 May 1828. The family home was at Dorset Place in Marylebone, London. George was a cadet at Addiscombe from 1847 to 1849, and joined the Bengal Artillery. He had been posted to Lucknow on 23 March as commandant of the 3rd Oudh Horse Field Battery.

A pair of medals were sold at auction in 2004 that belonged to Major B Ashe, Army of India, 1799–1826. These were the Burma Medal and Maharajpoor Star, 1843.

George Larkins was born on 5 October 1807 and was christened on 22 December at St Mary's Church in Lewisham; the son of John Larkins and his wife, Mary. He entered the Bengal Field Artillery and had reached the rank of major, in general charge of the artillery at Cawnpore, when the rebellion broke out.

George married Elizabeth, the daughter of a barrister named Thomas Cade Battley, and after she died he and Ewart 'Emma' (formerly Carnachan) were married in 1838. Emma was born at Stranraer, on 17 November 1808, the daughter of Robert Carnachan and his wife, Isabella (formerly Douglas).

Their three youngest surviving children were with them. Jessie Catherine Douglas was born in 1849; Emily Deborah was born in 1850; and George Lestock 'Georgie' was born in 1853, at Nynee Tal in West Bengal.

Four of their surviving children had been born in India but had been sent back to England for their education, and were being cared for at Elstree by Emma's cousin, Henrietta Coffin. They were: Constance Marion 'Connie' (1842–1916); Henry Thomas, who was born in 1843, at Meerut; Alice Schaffalitski (1846–1928); and Ellen Mona, who was born at Lucknow in 1847, and died in 1918.

Lieutenant Charles Dempster was born on 21 September 1826 at Buxar in Bengal, one of thirteen children to Doctor Thomas Erskine Dempster (born at St Andrews in Scotland in September 1799, died at 10 North Parade in Bath on 15 February 1883), and his wife Maria Christiana (formerly Innes). They had married at Benares in 1825. Doctor Dempster was the chief medical officer of the Bengal Horse Artillery, and he had served as medical officer with the 47th Bengal Native Infantry during the Barrackpore Mutiny of 1824, writing a descriptive account of the incident. He took part in the First Sikh War of 1845–46, and he was appointed superintendent of the field hospital during the Second Sikh War and the siege of Multan in 1848.

Charles had fought at Chillianwalla and Gujarat in the Second Sikh War, and was appointed adjutant of the 7th Battery, Bengal Artillery on 1 November 1853.

He married Jane Birrell at St Cuthbert's Church in Edinburgh on 16 April 1851, and they made their home at St Andrews in Fife. Jane was born at Cupar in Fife on 19 January 1832, the daughter of the Reverend John Birrell and his wife, Isabella (formerly Turner). Their four boys were born in India. Charles was born on 17 April 1852; William on 11 June 1853; Henry on 31 July 1855, and George on 20 February 1857.

Second Lieutenant George Maguire Wellington Sotheby was born at Secunderabad in India on 13 July 1837, the only son of Captain George Hull Sotheby (born in 1804) of the 34th Madras Light Infantry, who died in Hyderabad a year after he was born, and his wife, Catherine (formerly Lane, born in 1810). At the time of the 1841 census he was living in Crawley with his six-year-old sister, Georgina, and their great aunt, Sarah Lane. He was educated at college in Park Road, Hampton Wick.

His mother married Major Ralph John Thomas Williamson of the 1st Royal Lancashire Militia (born 1807). They were based at Crawley but they travelled much. With his father dead and his mother not around much, George decided to enter the Bengal Horse Artillery as soon as he was old enough. He was just nineteen years old when the Indian Rebellion broke out.

Gunner Sullivan was a member of the 1st Company, 6th Battalion, Bengal Artillery.

Commissariat

William Jonah Shepherd, known to his family as Jonah, was born in Allahabad in 1825, the third of four sons to James Shepherd (born at Burranpore in 1789), and his probably Indian wife. Thought of as a 'parade-ground bully,' in 1820 James was serving as a quartermaster-sergeant, and then as a regimental sergeant in the Bengal Army.

Described as a 'tall, earnest, and pious boy', Jonah was a champion of his religion, but also loved to listen to stories of his father's exploits, and those of his grandfather – 'a brawling adventurer'. By 1853 Jonah had become a head clerk with much influence in the large Commissariat and Ordnance Department in Cawnpore, and among the Eurasian community.

He met his wife, Ellen, a fifteen-year-old Eurasian girl, and they married in June 1850. In the following year they had a child named Polly, affectionately known as 'Bubba'. Jonah was well-aware that a darker skin brought restrictions to a person's progress in life, so he took great pains to describe his wife as 'fair' and of 'European parentage', and his child as 'fairer than native children'. He brought his sister to live with him, along with her infant son and two nieces, and the extended family moved to a house beside the old parade ground, across from Christ Church. There they employed an Ayah named Thakurani, who was completely devoted to them.

Conductor William Berrill was born in 1829 and married Ellen Margaret Fitzgerald at St John's Church in Cawnpore on 5 April 1851. Ellen was born in 1833. The family is referred to in Jonah Shepherd's account, where he stated that Mrs Berrill and her daughter were still capable of laughter, and referred to William as elderly. They were known to have two surviving sons named William and John Melville.

Medical Staff Corps

Before the Medical Staff Corps was formed in the Crimea in 1855, medical services were provided by a surgeon employed by the regiment to run a field hospital, usually staffed by soldiers acting as orderlies. On 1 August 1857 the MSC became the Army Hospital Corps.

Among the medical officers in India was Surgeon William Robert Boyes. He was born on 7 April 1815, and was christened at St Mary's Church in Lambeth, on 31 October 1816, with two other siblings named Frances and Rosetta, which suggests he was probably one of triplets. He was the son of William Boyes, an East India Company merchant, and his wife, Ann, of Brixton Hill in Surrey. William became a member of the Royal College of Surgeons (MRCS) and LSA on 25 May 1838, and a Fellow of the Royal College of Surgeons (FRCS) on 13 May 1857.

He married Catherine Mouat Biggs at Calcutta on 31 March 1845. His wife was known as Kate, the youngest daughter of General John Andrew Biggs (born in 1787) of the Bengal Artillery, and his wife, Barbara Mouat (born in 1793). A memorial at St Stephen's Church in Dum Dum dedicated to General Biggs states '… after serving his country for forty years, died at Cawnpore on 12 July 1844, aged 57 years'. At the time of the rebellion Doctor Boyes was serving as a medical officer with the 1st Bengal Native Infantry.

Assistant-Surgeon Thomas Godfrey Heathcote was born at Mansfield in Nottinghamshire on 15 March 1818. He was the son of Oakley Heathcote and his wife, Elizabeth (formerly Swymmer). His father was an insurance agent on the committee of the Northern Union. Thomas was the co-author of a book concerning the Andaman Islands. Thomas married Gertrude Lowther Sandham at St John's Cathedral in Calcutta on 20 February 1844. Gertrude had been born at Meerut on 21 June 1825, the daughter of Doctor Batkshell Lane Sandham, who died in 1848. She appears in the 1841 census as living in the home of Eliza Cheap at Stonefall in Bilton with Harrogate, with her sister Maria, and several other young people. Gertrude and Maria are both recorded as being aged fifteen on the document, which suggests they may have been twins.

Their father was appointed to the 58th (Rutlandshire) Regiment in June 1841, before transferring to the 16th Light Dragoons, and becoming first class staff surgeon in 1845. In 1843 Marian married Major Elliot D'Arcy Todd of the Bengal Artillery, who was killed in action during the Sutlej Campaign in the Punjab two years later. They had six children, with four other children seemingly back at school in England. They were Adeline Siddons, born in 1844; Henry Fisher, born in 1847; Annie, who lived most of her life in Canada, and Agnes Elizabeth, who was born in 1851 and is believed to have died young because she was not with her parents. With them in Cawnpore was Godfrey Swymmer, who had been born at Easthorpe in Southwell, Nottinghamshire, on 13 April 1854, and a new baby was born to them during the siege.

Bengal Native Forces

The regular cavalry established by the East India Company relied on the patronage of Indian rulers. In 1760 the first troops of Moghul Horse (rissalahs) to be raised were commanded by Sirdar Minza Shahbaz Khan (1st Horse) and Sirdar Khan Tar Beq (2nd Horse) and a third was raised in 1765. All three were disbanded in 1772.

Then in 1776 there were two regiments raised for the Nawab Wazir of Oudh and a third in 1776. The first two were disbanded in 1783 but the third continued as a troop for a while. A troop of Pathans was formed in 1778 and called the Kandahar Horse. In 1783 this and the third troop were raised up to regimental strength. The third troop became the 1st Regiment of Light Cavalry and the Kandahar Horse became the 2nd Regiment.

A third and fourth regiment were raised in the mid-1790s, four more in the early years of the nineteenth century and two more in 1825. The 11th was the last to be raised as late as 1842. The officers were British and the other ranks were Indian but all were dressed in British-style uniforms except for the other ranks' head-dress.

The force of about 33,000 men of the East India Company's Bengal Presidency Army, which was officered by British men, consisted of the 2nd Bengal Light Cavalry, and the 1st, 53rd and 56th Bengal Native Infantry, along with a company of their artillery.

2nd Bengal Native Cavalry

Major Edward Vibart was born at Amberd House in Pitminster near Taunton, on 15 November 1807, the son of Colonel James Meredith Vibart (1753–1827), and his wife Juliana (formerly Williams) who died in 1822. The Vibart family and the family of Captain Willie Halliday of the 56th were related.

Edward entered the service of the East India Company in 1825, joining the 2nd Bengal Light Cavalry. He had served at Ghazni during the First Anglo–Afghan War of 1839–42, and at Pannier during the Gwalior campaign of 1844.

At St Peter and St Paul Church in Bishops Hull in Taunton on 4 June 1833, Major Vibart married Emily, the daughter of Edward Coles and his wife, Louisa (formerly Hamilton), and they had a large family: Edward Daniel Hamilton (born 28 August 1837, died in 1923), Henrietta Louisa (born 20 December 1838, died 1926), Georgina Caroline (born 1 February 1844), Louisa Hamilton (born 23 April 1845), John Frances (born 1849), William Hamilton (born 21 March 1853) and Emily 'Emmie' (born Cawnpore in 1856).

Before the rebellion Edward junior, was a lieutenant in the 54th Bengal Native Infantry. He was stationed at Delhi, but in April 1857 he visited his parents in Cawnpore. He bid them goodbye early in May, not realising that it was the last time he would ever see them. Edward later wrote a chronicle of the violence committed by both sides, which was published in 1898.

Walter Albert Stirling was born at Perth in Australia in 1837, the fifth and youngest son in the family of eleven children to Admiral, Sir James Stirling (born Drumpellier in Lanarkshire on 28 January 1791, died Woodbridge, East Guildford, Surrey, on 22 April 1865), who was serving as the first governor of Australia, and his wife, Ellen (formerly Mangles, born Guildford on 3 September 1807, died London on 8 June 1874).

Walter came from a famous naval family, and his father saw service in the Napoleonic War of 1812, and in the Crimea, 1853–56. His sister, Georgina (christened at Bedhampton Church on 27 May 1845), was married to Major-General Sir Henry Tombs, who was awarded the Victoria Cross for gallantry at Delhi; and secondly to Major-General Sir Herbert Stewart, who commanded the troops during the expedition to try to rescue General Gordon at Khartoum. His mother was a daughter of James Mangles of Woodbridge (1762–1838), who was Member of Parliament for Guildford. She was related to Ross Lowis Mangles of the Bengal Civil Service, who was awarded the Victoria Cross for action at Arrah, becoming one of a very few number of civilians to be awarded the coveted medal.

Admiral Stirling was governor of Western Australia for a decade from 1829. He returned to England and on 19 August 1846, and he settled his family at Belmont, a large Georgian mansion in a large park in Bedhampton, near Havant in Hampshire, before moving to a house named Woodbridge in Guildford on 10 April 1860, where the Guildford

Grammar School now stands. Walter joined the Indian Army, and at the time of the siege he held the rank of cornet.

A detailed account of the history of the family appeared in the *Western Australian* of Perth on 20 June 1936.

Captain Robert Urquhart Jenkins was related to General Wheeler. He was born in 1828 in Calcutta, the second son of five children to Captain Robert Castle Jenkins, who was serving in the 61st Bengal Native Infantry when he married Anna Bassett Catherine, the daughter of John Palmer of Calcutta. Captain Jenkins was from Chepstow, and on leaving the army he became a successful merchant and was able to retire back to Beachley Manor and the family estate. Beachley is near Chepstow and in Gloucestershire. Robert Urquhart joined the 2nd Bengal Native Cavalry on 8 December 1845, and took part in the Sikh War of 1848–49. At the time of the rebellion he was captain in charge of Railway Engineers.

Captain Edward James Seppings had been born in Calcutta on 26 May 1826, the son of John Milligen Seppings (born Plymouth on 4 April 1798, died Torquay on 17 April 1863) who was inspector of shipping for the East India Company at Calcutta for twenty years. His mother was Marianne Matthews (formerly Ellis, born in 1796, died Torquay on 16 August 1853). He had a sister named Charlotte Marianne (born in Calcutta on 2 March 1823, died in 1894), and a brother named Robert Seymour, who was described as an invalid and died in 1881.

His grandfather was Sir Robert Seppings, a well-known naval architect, who had lived in Holt Road, Fakenham, and began his working life as a shipwright in the Plymouth dockyard. He retired to live at 3 Mount Terrace in Taunton in 1832, where he died in 1840. His grandparents were first cousins, and his grandmother was Charlotte Milligen (1770–1834).

Captain Seppings' wife, Jessie, was a Scottish girl, born at South Leith on 20 February 1826, and christened at St Cuthbert's Church in Edinburgh on 18 August 1834 as an eight-year-old. She was the daughter of Adam Ogilvie Turnbull (born 12 January 1796, died 18 July 1835) and Margaret Somerville (born in May 1810). Her father had been a builder of South Leith near Edinburgh with the company of David McGibbon and A. O. Turnbull, who, among many architectural projects, built the customs house at Leith Docks. Her father died at Briery Hole in Roxburghshire when Jessie was ten. As a young woman she went out to India with her uncle, who had been a surgeon in Scotland.

Jessie and Captain Seppings became a couple and they married at the India Office in Bengal on 20 November 1849. They had two fair-haired boys named John James, who was born in 1852, and Edward Matthew, who was born in 1854, and a newborn male infant.

Lieutenant Francis Stoneham Montagu Wren was born in 1836 and was baptised at St Margaret's Church in Northam near Bideford, Devon, on 18 November 1836. He was the youngest son of Major Thomas Wren (1781–1870) of Lenwood House in Northam, and his wife Delitia Montagu (born in 1794), the youngest daughter of Admiral Barton of Burrough in Devon. Admiral Barton was a descendant of the Leigh family, made famous by Charles Kingsley in his classic novel *Westward Ho!* Major Wren had retired from the Madras Army and was a DL and JP, and a landowner, being described as: '… a locally social prominent.' Delitia died on 17 June 1836 (the same year as Francis was born), and his older brother, Henry Conway, died aged fifteen on 12 August 1838. Francis was educated at Bideford Grammar School and at the Reverend Rowsell's School in Stepney.

Wren's father nominated him to Major James Oliphant for a cadetship in the Bengal Cavalry, who in turn nominated him to the authorities at Addiscombe on 7 February 1854, and he passed the military committee at East India House in London the next day. He was appointed cornet on 4 April 1854, and on deciding to take the overland route to India, he set off on the same day, travelling via Marseilles and the Suez Canal, and he arrived in Calcutta on 15 May. He was directed to do duty from 6 June with the 1st Bengal Light Cavalry, before being transferred to the 2nd Bengal Light Cavalry stationed at Cawnpore on 7 August. He was promoted lieutenant a year later, and on 1April 1856 he passed the examination in colloquial Hindustani.

Lieutenant Murray George Daniell was born at Carshalton in Surrey (now a suburb of the London borough of Sutton) on 10 September 1836 and was baptised at All Saints Church at Carshalton on the same day. He was the third son in the family of eleven children to Captain Edward Maxwell Daniell, RN, of the East India Company (born Marylebone in London on 19 February 1798, died Offam House in Sussex on 2 October 1862) formerly of Gloucester Square, Hyde Park, London, and his wife, Emma Isabella (formerly Ferrers, born London in 1803, died Sussex Square, Hyde Park, London, on 4 December 1882). She came from a family of London shippers of the East India Company, and Captain Daniell was in command of many of their ships going out to Bengal and China.

Captain Daniell owned land in County Wexford, Ireland. Lieutenant Daniell was described as 'Brave to admiration, a fearless horseman, foremost in all field sports, and universally beloved for his great amiability.'

Lieutenant John Hammond Harrison was born at Barham, near Canterbury in Kent, on 2 October 1832, the fourth son in a family of eight children to Benjamin Harrison (born Portugal on 12 May 1792, died 31 January 1865) of Blackheath Park, who was in the service of the Madras Civil Service, and his wife, Charlotte Mary (born 21 October 1794, died 3 November 1876), the daughter of the Reverend Anthony Egerton Hammond, the rector of Knowlton and Ivychurch, Romney Marsh in Kent, and his wife Charlotte (formerly Biggs).

Lieutenant Melville Balfour was born on 30 September 1838, the fourth son in a family of seven children of Charles Balfour (1786–1870), a merchant, of Lower Berkeley Street in Mayfair, London, and Maria Caroline (formerly Harington, 1803–76). He was baptised at St Mary's Church in Marylebone, London, on 23 November 1838. He was educated at the recently established Radley College in Oxfordshire from 1848 to 1852, and afterwards attended Bradfield Boarding School in Berkshire. He entered the Indian Army in 1855.

Lieutenants Charles William Quinn and Richard Owen Quinn were the sons of Captain Thomas Quinn, 4th Bengal Light Cavalry, who died on 7 November 1857. They were born at Meerut, and joined the Bengal Army in 1846 aged twenty-eight.

1st Bengal Native Infantry

This was the first locally recruited unit of the East India Company forces. It had been raised by Robert Clive himself at Calcutta in 1757 as Lal Pultan (Red Battalion), ranked as 1st Battalion, but was also known by its members as Gillies' Pultan, after Captain Primrose Gillies. The unit was present at the battle of Plassey on 26 June 1757.

The establishment of Bengal Native Infantry at the time of the rebellion usually consisted of ten companies of about 100 men in each. There was a European in overall command, a European adjutant, quartermaster, and occasionally some additional staff officers. Each company had a European officer, two native officers and six native non-commissioned officers.

After three months of forced marches of about 15 miles a day, the unit had arrived at Cawnpore in February 1857 from Cuttack in the southwest of Bengal.

Colonel John Ewart was a member of an old border family dating back to 1370. He was born at the Moseley Street Presbyterian Church in Manchester on 27 July 1803, the eldest of five sons in a family of seven children of Peter Ewart (born 14 May 1767), an influential engineer and cotton merchant in Manchester, who was one of eleven children to a Church of Scotland minister from Dumfries, and his wife, Marianne (formerly Kerr) of Edinburgh, who had married in the Scottish capital on 16 September 1800.

John was christened at the Unitarian Chapel on Upper Brook Street in Manchester a month later. One of his cousins was Lieutenant-General John Frederick Ewart CB of the 67th Regiment, who found fame in the Peninsula campaigns, and his son, John's cousin, was General, Sir John Alexander Ewart GCB, who was a senior officer with the 93rd Highlanders during the famous 'Thin Red Line' action at Balaclava in the Crimea, and the capture of Lucknow.

Peter Ewart was influential in the development of turbines and the theories of thermodynamics. He was trained by the company set up by Matthew Boulton and James Watt to produce their advanced steam engines, and Peter helped to erect the first steam engine to be used in a textile mill at Quarry Bank in Cheshire. He was a member of the

Manchester branch of the Literary and Philosophical Society from 1786, becoming vice-president in 1812, writing a paper for the society entitled 'The Measure of Moving Force'. Peter took up a post working for the Admiralty in 1835. He was killed in a terrible accident when a chain snapped and he was crushed while he was supervising the removal of a boiler at the Woolwich Dock Yard on 15 September 1842.

The industrial metropolis of Manchester had recently become a city. The Free Trade Hall was completed in 1857 after three years of construction at Peter's Field, the site of the infamous Peterloo Massacre. On a 3-acre site at Old Trafford, a large fine arts exhibition was opened by Prince Albert on 5 May 1857, entitled 'The Art Treasures of Great Britain', which included paintings by the British 'modern masters' of William Hogarth, John Constable, Joseph Turner and Thomas Gainsborough, as well as photographs taken in the Crimea by James Robertson. Around 1.3 million people attended the exhibition until it closed on 17 October 1857, and it remains one of the largest such events ever to be held anywhere in the world.

Coming from such a distinguished military family, it was not surprising that John Ewart chose the army as a career. As he rose through the ranks he became fluent in several local languages, acting as interpreter to a number of regiments from 1835. He took command of the 1st Bengal Native Infantry in 1855, becoming known as 'a strict parade-ground disciplinarian' who apparently addressed his men as his 'children'. Mowbray Thomson described him as 'a brave and clever man'. John married Emma Sophia, one of sixteen children of Thomas Broadley Fooks (1774–1840), and his wife, Maria Penelope (1789–1850, formerly Cracroft). Her father was a solicitor and clerk to the court of requests, as were several of her brothers. Emma was baptised at Dartford in Kent on 11 December 1818. They had a two-year-old daughter named Agnes Emma.

Emma was a woman who had come to know India well and had learned to accept the service life of her husband and the duties demanded of her. She wrote three letters home to her sister, Frances Jane, known as Fanny, which gave a good insight into the feelings of the people of Cawnpore as fears for their uncertain future grew.

Captain Athill Turner was born on 8 October 1819 at Toxteth Park in Liverpool, the fifth son in the large family of Charles Turner and his wife, Maria (formerly Athill). He was baptised on 9 December 1819 at St George's Church in Derby Square, Liverpool. His father was a West India merchant of London and Liverpool, who owned the Lynch Estate on the Caribbean island of Antigua. The family home was at 21 South Hill Place, Toxteth Park in Liverpool. Maria died in 1841 and Charles died in 1854. They are buried at St Michael's Church in Toxteth. They had several boys born in Liverpool, and one of Captain Turner's siblings, Edward Tindal, became the registrar of Oxford University.

Liverpool was still only a town before 1857, but its dock area was second only to London in capacity. Private companies had begun to provide piped water to some residents, but poor people still had to rely in filling barrels at wells until 1857, when a municipal water supply was begun.

On 18 November 1852, at Rawalpindi, Captain Turner married Ellen, the daughter of Reverend Richard Pain DCL (1774–1854), and his wife, Elizabeth (formerly Fisher, 1779–1858). Ellen had been born at Aspley Guise near Woburn in Bedfordshire on Christmas Day 1823 and had been baptised in 20 January 1824. They had James, born at Peshawar on 30 August 1853, Ellen Elizabeth, born on 10 May 1855, and Maria Edith, born on 5 May 1857. The two girls died at Cawnpore on 10 May 1857, Maria being only five days old.

It has been suggested that Ellen Turner, aged forty-eight, and her daughter, Ellen, who lived in a cottage in the High Street at Bushey in Hertfordshire during the 1871 census, are Mrs and Miss Turner. Ellen senior is recorded as being a widow, born in The Strand in London, and Ellen junior is stated to have been born at Bow Street in London. Her age is given as twenty-one, which makes her year of birth as about 1850, two years before her parents were married.

The 1891 census records James Turner as living in the vicarage at Ingleton near Skipton in Yorkshire. He is described as aged thirty-seven, and was a clerk in holy orders, vicar of Ingleton.

Captain Edward John Elms was born in Itchingfield Vicarage near Horsham in 1823, and was baptised at Itchingfield, West Sussex, on 23

November of that year. He was the oldest son in a large family of the late Reverend Edward Elms (born 1786, died 3 May 1845) of St Nicolas Church, Itchingfield, and his wife, Jane Elizabeth (formerly Wyndham, born 1794, died 3 July 1870). He had two older sisters, of whom Emma had been born in Fulham in 1816, and had married John Stileman Bostock at Itchingfield on 22 September 1840.

At Ipswich in July 1852, Edward married Dorcas Guyon Boys, the daughter of the Reverend John Garwood Bull and Catherine Martha (formerly Smith). Their only child, Florence Helen, was born on 22 June 1853, at Peshawar in India. Sadly, Dorcas died soon after the birth on 4 July 1853, at Peshawar.

Lieutenant Frederick Redman was born in 1831, at 71 East India Dock Road in Poplar, London, the youngest of four sons of George Clavering Redman. His father was a successful merchant and ship owner, who by 1836 had warehouses near the West India Docks, a counting house and warehouses in Lime Street, a fleet of a dozen sailing ships and a seat on the board of a steamboat company. He was also a deputy-lieutenant at the Tower of London. The family motto was: *si ne sanguine nulla trophea* – which roughly translated means: *Without blood there is no victory.*

By about 1853, Redman's father had retired to live at Claringbold House near Broadstairs, Isle of Thanet in Kent, and his third son, Stephen, took over his shipping affairs.

Redman's brother, the second son, George Clavering Redman (1821–76), had served with the Kaiser Nicholas Imperial Cuirassier Guard of Austria, subsequently of the cavalry of the German Auxiliary Legion during the Crimean War, and late a lieutenant in the 7th (Princess Royal's) Regiment of Dragoon Guards while stationed in the Punjab, India.

13th Bengal Native Infantry

Adam Montague Turnbull was born in Calcutta in 1821, the son of P. Turnbull, the appraiser at Calcutta Custom House, and he joined the service of the East India Company in 1842.

16th Bengal Native Infantry

Lieutenant Frederick Cortlandt Angelo was born at Kurnaul in India on 6 October 1826, the son of Frederick John Joseph Angelo (1800–69) and his wife, Catherine Ogden (formerly Anderson, 1802–63). He was educated by Doctor Grieg at Walthamstow House School in north London, and at Addiscombe College from 1843 to 1844.

After his education he was fully prepared for service with the East India Company, and on his return to India he became attached to the 50th Bengal Native Infantry on 14 March 1845. He was appointed ensign with the 16th Bengal Native Infantry on 10 February 1846, being promoted lieutenant on 6 January 1850.

While Angelo was serving with the 50th he suffered an unfortunate fall from grace and was tried by court martial on 25 October 1847 on a charge of 'unbecoming conduct in having detained in his possession certain ornaments belonging to a native woman, who died when under Ensign Angelo's protection and having repeatedly declined delivering them up to the parents of the deceased; of having severely beaten with a stick the brother and mother of the said deceased; and in having conducted himself with great disrespect to his commanding officer, Lieutenant-Colonel Gardner.'

He was acquitted of the first instance of the charge and found guilty of the remainder with the exception of the words 'mother' and 'great', of which the court acquitted him. He was sentenced to be publicly and severely reprimanded.

Angelo was appointed lieutenant on 6 January 1850, and on 31 October that year, at St Mary's Church in Benares, he married Helena Elizabeth Gordon (formerly Cumming, born 1817), and they had two daughters, Helena Adelaide Cortlandt, who was born at Etawah in India on 22 June 1853, and Catherine Cortlandt, who was born at Etawah in 1854.

Helena was pregnant with their third child when Angelo was seconded to the department of public works, and appointed superintendent 4th (terminal) division on the Ganges Canal at Cawnpore on 14 May 1857. He had arrived at Cawnpore with his pregnant wife and his young daughters, and they were living on a boat on the river.

31st Bengal Native Infantry

Colonel Alexander Jack CB, of the 31st Bengal Native Infantry, was born on 19 October 1805, one of four sons of the late Reverend William Jack and his wife, Grace. His father was sub-principal of the University and King's College in Aberdeen from 1800 to 1815, and principal from 1815 until his death on 9 February 1854. His mother was the daughter of Andrew Bolt from Lerwick in the Shetlands. He was a student of mathematics and philosophy at his father's college from 1820 to 1822, and was remembered as 'a tall, handsome, soldierly young man'.

Jack was appointed cadet in the Bengal Army in 1823, and was appointed ensign in the late 30th Bengal Native Infantry on 23 May 1824. He became lieutenant on 30 August 1825, captain on 2 December 1832, and major on 19 June 1846. He was present with his battalion at the battle of Aliwal during the First Sikh War, and at Chillianwala and Gujarat during the Second Sikh War. His brother, Andrew William Thomas Jack, was visiting him from Australia when the Indian Rebellion broke out.

41st Bengal Native Infantry

Captain William Williamson was born in Scotland in 1824, the son of Major-General David Williamson, who was in the service of the Honourable East India Company. Captain Williamson had seen active service in the Sutlej and Punjab campaigns, for which he received medals and clasps. He was serving as Deputy-Assistant Commissary General. His wife, Jessie, and infant daughter, Eleanor, were with him at Cawnpore.

48th Bengal Native Infantry

Gilbert Ironside Bax was born in 1833, the third son of five in the family of seven children to John Bax (born Faversham, Kent, in 1793, died Wiesbaden, Germany, on 22 July 1863) of the Indian Civil Service, who later became a JP for Hertfordshire and lived at Twyford House in Thorley near Bishop Stortford. His mother was Jane (formerly Ironside, born 2 July 1807 at Houghton-le-Spring in Durham, died on 3 April 1878 at Ryde, Isle of Wight). They had married on 4 September 1826 in Thorley. Gilbert received a commission as a lieutenant in the 48th Bengal Native Infantry.

53rd Bengal Native Infantry

The 53rd was raised in 1804 as the 1st Battalion, 27th Regiment of Bengal Native Infantry, and in 1824 became known as the 53rd Regiment of Bengal Native Infantry, under the command of Major J. Canning.

The unit arrived at Cawnpore in February 1857. Captain Mowbray Thomson described them as

> '… a fine regiment, about a thousand strong, almost all of them Oudh men, averaging five feet eight inches in height; their uniform the old British red, with yellow facings. By far the greater number of them being high caste men, they were regarded by the native populace as very aristocratic and stylish gentlemen … Thoroughly disciplined and martial in appearance, these native troops provided one memorable point of contrast with European forces – drunkenness was altogether unknown amongst them.'

Mowbray Thomson was born at Agra in India, on 1 April 1832, the son of Richard Marten Mowbray Thomson (born Hamilton, Scotland, on 17 April 1799), a surgeon in the East India Company, who took part in the storming of the Ghuznee fort in Afghanistan on 23 July 1839. Mowbray's paternal grandparents were Captain Andrew Thomson and his wife Barbara (formerly Hamilton). Surgeon Thomson died on 23 March 1848, and was buried in Bengal. Mowbray's mother, Mary Josephine, was an accountant who had been born in Ceylon in 1806, and he had a sister named Eliza who had also been born in Agra in the year after Mowbray. Mary came back to England in the year after her husband died, and the family home at the time of the Indian Rebellion was 34 Pembridge Villas, Westbourne Grove in Bayswater, west London. On the 1851 census the portrait painter James Sant was a visitor at the house, and they had three servants. Eliza eventually married Sant.

Like Lieutenant Angelo, Mowbray Thomson was educated at Walthamstow House in Leytonstone. According to the *Annual Register* 'He went out to Calcutta for mercantile life while still a boy.' Mowbray had entered the 53rd Bengal Native Infantry in December 1853 and at the time of the rebellion he had been appointed captain. He was described as having 'the bright face and laughing eyes of an undergraduate in his first term'.

Lieutenant Gilbert Augustus Masters was Captain Thomson's twenty-five-year old friend. Thomson told the story of how, in December 1856, he and Masters were stationed in Cuttack in the extreme south-west of Bengal, and they went bear-hunting for a few weeks 'Robinson Crusoe style', in the rocky mountains and thick jungles in the region. During this time Captain Thomson was attacked by a bear. He wounded the beast but it clawed and injured him.

Masters was the son of Lieutenant-Colonel Robert A. Masters, who commanded the 7th Bengal Light Cavalry. Colonel Masters was stationed in the Lucknow area and on 31 May 1857, after a pre-arranged signal, most of his troopers mutinied at the Mudkipur cavalry lines a few miles from the Lucknow Residency and deserted to the rebels. Loyal native infantry, commanded by Sir Henry Lawrence, eventually dispersed them. The sabretache he used at Lucknow is preserved in the National Army Museum.

Lieutenant Henry George de la Fosse was born in Lucknow on 24 April 1835 and was baptised at Fatehgarh. He had at least five sisters, and was the son of Major Henry de la Fosse of the Bengal Artillery, who was born on 11 March 1794 at Richmond in Surrey, and his wife, Louisa Maria (formerly Shield), who was born at Northampton in 1808, and worked as an accountant. A portrait of Major de la Fosse in his uniform still exists. It was taken in 1842, bearing the address of The Promenade in Cheltenham. Major de la Fosse died at Ferozepore while on active service in the First Anglo–Sikh War in the Punjab, on 3 October 1845.

Described as 'pale and wiry', Henry was educated at Marlborough College (the first headmaster being a brother-in-law of his mother), at Nelson House School in Wimbledon, which an uncle-in-law, John Brackenbury, later established as a military academy, and at the East India Company Military College at Addiscombe in Surrey. He entered the Indian Army in 1854 and served with the 53rd Bengal Native Infantry, but he seems to have been attached to the Bengal Artillery during the siege of Cawnpore.

Lieutenant-Colonel Stephen Williams was the fifty-two-year-old son of Henry Williams, who had been a merchant in the civil service of the East India Company, based at Howrah in the suburbs of Calcutta, before his death in 1836. He had married Mary Blanchard Bray, and they had three daughters, Mary, Georgina and Frances.

The 56th Bengal Native Infantry

The 56th formed part of General Gough's 'Army of the Sutlej' during the First Anglo–Sikh War of 1845–46, and the 'Army of the Punjab' in the Second War of 1849, taking part in the final battle of Gujarat in 1849.

Ensign Robert Allen Stevens was born at Wilmington in Dartford, Kent, and he was baptised in the town on 20 May 1839. He was the third of four sons in the family of seven children (the first child died in infancy) of the Reverend Henry Stevens MA, who at that time was the vicar of St Michael and Al Angels Church at Wilmington, and his wife, Mary Frances (born at the Royal Arsenal in Woolwich, London in 1805), the daughter of Colonel Charles Cox Bingham (1772–1835) of the Royal Artillery. Reverend Stevens had been born in London on 29 November 1808, and he and Mary were married at St James's Church in Piccadilly, London, by his father, Robert Stevens, the Dean of Rochester, on 10 September 1833.

A memorial in Wilmington churchyard is dedicated to 'Charles Halsey Stevens, infant son of the Reverend Henry Stevens, vicar of this parish, died 1 June 1840'. The tragic event is likely to have been the reason why they moved to another church, and soon afterwards Henry became the vicar of St John the Baptist Church at Wateringbury near Maidstone in Kent, where he remained until his death in the vicarage on 22 October 1877. The family lived in the vicarage throughout this time.

Captain William Leonard 'Willie' Halliday was born on 9 September 1821, at Chapel Cleeve near Maidenhead in Somerset, the third son in the family of seven children to John Halliday (1791–1826) and Ann Innes (formerly Dyer). The Halliday family, and the family of Major Vibart of the 2nd Cavalry were related. On 20 July 1852, at West Lodge, Iwerne Minster, near Blandford in Dorset, Captain Halliday married Emma Laetitia (formerly Wyndham); which was Emma's home. Their only child, Edith Mabel, was born at Chapel Cleeve in 1853.

Emma was born in 1833, at West Lodge, the second oldest of eight children to Captain Alexander Wadham Wyndham of the Scots Greys (born 1800 at Ditton, Wiltshire, died 1869 at Wilton in Wiltshire), and his wife, Emma (formerly Trevelyan, born 27 February 1801 at Nettlecombe, Dorset, died 17 May 1869 at Shaftesbury in Wiltshire). They married in London on 22 June 1830, and lived at West Lodge; they also owned Burrishoole House and Estates in County Mayo, Ireland.

There is a story that while Emma was walking in the Dorset countryside at Cranborne Chase near Blandford she met a gypsy woman. The Romany told her some things about how her life would progress, including that she would be taken to 'a far off country across the seas' and there meet a 'terrible' death!

She was known as a zealous Christian. She had the Bible printed in Urdu and Devanagari and had it distributed among the sepoys. This greatly raised their suspicions that the British were intent on converting them to Christianity.

Captain Halliday had seen action with the 56th as part of the Army of the Punjab, and he and Emma had become acquainted with Edward and Jessie Seppings while they were both stationed at Neemuch. Before the rebellion, Major Vibart and his wife often entertained Captains Halliday and Seppings and their wives at their home. They all had connections in the West Country.

Lieutenant Henry John Gregory Warde was born on 3 July 1837, the son of Rear-Admiral Charles Warde (1786–1869) JP and KH (Knight of Hanover), of Preswylfa, Neath in Glamorganshire.

Lieutenant Hornby Fagan was a member of an ancient family of Cork, being born at Feltrim, Knockrea in County Cork, on 7 May 1833. He was the son of William Trant Fagan (1801–59), and his wife Mary, the daughter of Charles Addis. His father was a landowner and mayor of Cork in 1844, who was Member of Parliament for Cork, 1847–51 and 1852–59. He wrote *The Life and Times of Daniel O'Connell* in 1847. Hornby had older brothers named Charles (1829–1903), and William (1832–90); and a younger sister named Mary (1838–88). William became a captain with the 12th Lancers, and Member of Parliament for Carlow between 1869 and 1874.

Ensign John Wright Henderson and his brother Robert William served with the 7nd Bengal Light Infantry. They were the two eldest sons of the Reverend Robert Henderson MA, who was the incumbent of the Holy Trinity Episcopal Church at Wellington Place, St Ninians in Stirling for forty years. Robert was born in about 1836, John in about 1838, and they were both educated at Glenalmond and at University College, Oxford.

Chapter 4

Life in the Mid-1850s

The world was progressing swiftly during the mid-nineteenth century. Engineers were preparing the first plans for the construction of the Suez Canal, which considerably cut short the time it took to get from Britain to India, and Isambard Kingdom Brunel was preparing the SS *Great Eastern* for its launch. It was towards the end of 1857 when Robert Howlett took the famous photograph of the cigar-smoking Brunel standing before the massive launching chains of his great ship at Millwall Docks.

Three great universities of India were founded in 1857. The Calcutta (Kolkata) University Act came into force on 24 January 1857, the University of Bombay (Mumbai) was established by Sir Charles Wood and opened on 18 July 1857, and the University of Madras (Chennai) was founded on 5 September 1857.

The study of tropical diseases was also making steady progress. Three days after the Indian rebellion broke out at Meerut, Ronald Ross was born at Almora, about 180 miles away. He was the eldest of ten children to a general in the army of the East India Company, and as such was sent home to the Isle of Wight to live with his aunt and uncle. He went on to become a medical doctor and the first British Nobel laureate, which he achieved for Physiology and Medicine in 1902, for his work in studying the transmission of malaria.

Auguste Ambroise Tardieu was undertaking his pioneering work on forensic medicine and toxicology at the University of Paris. In 1857 he published his book, *Medical-Legal Studies of Sexual Assault*, which was the first work to be put into the public domain that specifically studied child abuse.

By the mid-1850s most of the seasonal festivities we still enjoy had already been established. The Christmas of 1856 was the last Christmas the victims of the Cawnpore tragedy would have enjoyed. The vision of

Santa Claus in a red suit and white beard coming down the chimney to leave gifts was introduced by the poem commonly known as '*Twas the Night Before Christmas*, which had been published in 1823, and Charles Dickens' *A Christmas Carol* had been available since Christmas 1843. The tradition of decorating a Christmas tree was common practice by 1857, the pulling of Christmas crackers had been enjoyed since being introduced in about 1850, and plum pudding was traditionally served at the end of the Christmas dinner. In autumn 1857, James Lord Pierpont (1822–93) of Boston, Massachusetts, copyrighted and published his *One Horse Open Sleigh*, originally written for the Thanksgiving season, but it was later adopted as a Christmas song with the title *Jingle Bells*. In 1965 it became the first song broadcast from outer space. In 1855, another Bostonian, John Sullivan Dwight, had translated from the original French version into English the beautiful Christmas song, *O Holy Night*, which was then and still is a Christmas classic.

Literature prior to the mid-Victorian era focused mainly on works for preaching and instruction. Since about 1700 children had been brought up on the alphabet poem that began 'A was an archer who shot at a frog'. *Hymns for Little Children* by Cecil Frances Alexander appeared in 1848 and contained three hymns renowned throughout the English-speaking world – *Once in Royal David's City*, *There Is a Green Hill Far Away* and *All Things Bright and Beautiful*. Some books written for adults such as *Gulliver's Travels* were read by the young. Stories of real children thinking childlike thoughts and getting into childhood scrapes in which child readers could recognise their own behaviour began to make their mark in the mid-nineteenth century, such as Charlotte Yonge's *The Daisy Chain* written for older girls and published in 1856.

Aesop's *The Tortoise and the Hare*, the stories of the Arabian Nights including *Ali Baba* and *Aladdin*; and Charles Perrault's collection of folk tales including *The Sleeping Beauty* and *Cinderella* had long been available; Grimm's Fairy Tales including *Snow White*, *Hansel and Gretel* and *Rapunzel* had been published in 1812; and the limericks of Edward Lear and his poem *The Owl and the Pussycat* would also have been familiar by 1857. Other popular juvenile verse included *Twinkle, Twinkle Little Star* (1806); *Mary Had a Little Lamb* (1830); *The Spider and the Fly* (1834); *Wee Willy Winkie* (1841) and *The Pied Piper of Hamelin* (1842).

Several still well-known books were published in 1857, including *Little Dorrit* by Charles Dickens, and *Tom Brown's Schooldays* by Thomas Hughes. Among the characters is Flashman, a bully who torments Tom. The character was adopted by George MacDonald Fraser as the narrator for his series entitled *The Flashman Papers*. The fifth instalment entitled *Flashman in the Great Game*, published in 1875, tells the fictional story of his experiences during the Indian Mutiny and how he survived the Siege of Cawnpore.

During the nineteenth century most toys had to be of an educational nature, either academic or ecclesiastical. Factory-made items, including tin and clockwork toys, went on sale. Rich children had more toys to choose from, such as train sets, toy soldiers, rocking horses, dolls and dolls houses, tea sets and toy shops with fruit, vegetables, meat, hats and medicine. Other popular toys were alphabet bricks, sailing boats, jigsaw puzzles (or dissections as they were known until about 1880), and models of Noah's Ark. In many homes children were not allowed to play with toys on Sundays – except Noah's Ark, because that was in the Bible.

In the world of music the composer Edward Elgar was born near Worcester on 2 June 1857 and his *Nimrod* from the *Enigma Variations* is played at every Trooping of the Colour held at Horse Guards Parade in Whitehall. The Panopticon Music Hall was opened in Glasgow in 1857, and many years later Stan Laurel was to make his debut there. Weston's Music Hall was opened in Holborn in London later in the year, which would eventually be known as the popular Holborn Empire. The reading room at the British Museum was opened on 18 May 1857.

In April 1857 Queen Victoria invited Leonida Caldesi to Buckingham Palace to photograph the royal children, and on 26 May Caldesi took the well-known group portrait photograph of the royal family on the terrace at Osborne House on the Isle of Wight, which included all nine of Queen Victoria's children. She celebrated her birthday on 24 May; as most of the British people of Cawnpore were straggling into the entrenchment. The last full week of June 1857 was a busy one for the sovereign. On 22 June she opened the new building that housed the South Kensington Museum, later renamed the Victoria and Albert Museum; which had its origins in the Great Exhibition of 1851; on 25 June she held a ceremony at which she formally granted the title of Prince Consort to her husband, Albert;

and on 26 June in Hyde Park, she presented the first sixty-two Victoria Crosses to veterans of the Crimean War. She arrived in Manchester on 29 June to visit the Art Treasures of Great Britain Exhibition, and remained there for two days.

The mid-1850s were pioneering years in the world of sport. In Sheffield during the summer of 1857 two cricketers named Nathaniel Creswick and William Priest were busy organising informal kickabouts and trying to convince other members of the Sheffield Cricket Club that they should form a football section, and the world's first football club – Sheffield FC – was established at a meeting in a greenhouse a few months later. That year also saw the foundation of Liverpool (St Helens) FC, the rugby union club that is said to be the oldest open rugby club in the world.

With the help of the expansion of the railways, the first cricket match between two travelling teams took place in 1857 between the All-England Eleven (AEE) and the United All-England Eleven (UEE), and came to be considered as the most important of the English season until 1866. Cricket is now the most popular sport in India.

On 4 March 1857 a horse named Emigrant, trained and ridden by Charlie Boyce, won the Grand National at Aintree in Liverpool, and on 1 June 1857 a horse named Blink Bonny won the Derby at Epsom for a prize of £5,700 – which is the equivalent of £3,640,000 today, and returned to Epsom two days later to win the Oaks. On 16 June 1857, Tom Sayers won a gruelling eighty-five-round bare-knuckle fight against William Perry to become the British champion. Perry was so seriously injured that he retired after the fight.

France and Great Britain had traditionally been great enemies, including in India during the previous century. However, they formed another Alliance as they had done in the Crimea and formally declared war on China on 3 March 1857, to start the Second Opium War. 4 April 1857 marked the end of the Anglo–Persian War.

India was the first tropical country where British women went to live, and large numbers of wives, daughters and sisters of East Indian Company officials, military men and civil servants had been accompanying or joining their men in India since the 1760s. Some even went for sheer adventure, or were part of 'The Fishing Fleet' – the

name given to women who went out to India's 'happy hunting ground'
to look for a husband.

Emily Eden accompanied her brother, Lord George Auckland, the
governor-general of India, on a tour of the north-west regions in 1837–
38, mainly to secure the support of the Sikh leader, Ranjit Singh. They
arrived at Cawnpore on 21 December 1837, and writing on New Year's
Day of 1838 she recorded in a letter to her sister Eleanor back in London:

> The dust at Cawnpore has been quite dreadful the last two days.
> People lose their way on the plains. It is here, too, that we first came
> into the starving districts. They have had no rain for a year and a
> half, the cattle all dead, and the people all dying or gone away …
> the distress is perfectly dreadful. You cannot conceive the horrible
> sights we see, particularly children; perfect skeletons in many cases,
> their bones through their skin, without a rag of clothing, and utterly
> unlike human creatures … G and I walked down to the stables
> before breakfast this morning, and found such a miserable little
> baby, something like an old donkey, but with glazed, stupid eyes,
> under the care of another little wretch of about six years old. I am
> sure you would have sobbed to see the way the little atom flew at a
> cup of milk … and the way in which the little brother fed it. Doctor
> D says it cannot live, it is so diseased with starvation, but I mean to
> try what can be done for it.

Note she used the word 'it' to describe another human being.

These women were mainly of the middle and upper classes, accustomed
to the pleasant well-ordered life of the town house and country estate.
They were not used to hard lives, so took as much as they could that
would reflect the way they had lived and create their own little Britain
in the tropics. The journey was made relatively easy by good planning,
but it must still have been a daunting one for they packed as many home
comforts as they could, such as the sofa, the wash stand, the chest of
drawers and the looking-glass.

Ladies were recommended to take three pairs of corsets (known as
stays), which must have been torture to wear on the journey in a congested
cabin as the ship rolled on rough seas, and particularly beneath the hot

tropical sun. Women were taught that they must always dress indoors as if they were going out into the company of others just in case of a surprise visitor, so for the Well-Bred woman there was little possibility of removing them, and they had to suffer in silence.

During the voyage the women had to reflect on what would have to be done for their children. By the time the children were seven, or even younger, they would have to go back to Britain because a British education was considered essential. The mothers would have to reconcile themselves with a painful separation, unless they decided to travel back with their children. However, this meant leaving a husband who might, and often did, seek consolation from an Indian mistress. Some had no choice but to leave their children behind when they left home, sometimes in the hands of nannies who they had only recently employed for the duty and were complete strangers.

Many new arrivals in India could draw comfort from their appearance and their fashionable wardrobes. However, the dreadful heat of the Indian climate dictated how they led their lives. Clothes rotted and disintegrated because of the humidity, and termites that thrived in the dank climate could even destroy the foundations of a house overnight. Bouts of fever soon turned their pink and white complexions to pallid yellow. During the height of the hot weather people had to get up as early as possible before the sun rose just to fit in a quick side-saddle horse ride before breakfast. Between breakfast and lunch it was impossible to do any kind of energetic activity. A little sewing was about as much as could be accomplished, being confined in their rooms protected from the sun by pumas that continually broke and fell off their fixings. This was all they could manage until the happy hour of about 5:30 pm, when the sun at last began to go down and it was possible to tolerate a carriage drive before dinner. Even a breeze gave no respite as it usually blew hot and dry. Until the cold season every manual task was removed from the lady's hands by her train of servants. Even a relatively modest establishment could not function without at least a cook, scullion, sweeper, water-carrier, washerman, maid and outdoor staff.

This restricted lifestyle caused much boredom, and it was to fill these tedious idle hours that most women took to writing long diaries and letters to friends and family back home, which give a remarkably complete picture of their lives. Other strictly feminine pursuits were sketching, painting, playing cards and making music on pianos, the tone of which had been ruined by the hot climate. Pastimes were strictly limited to most ladies. They attended and gave private balls, and amateur theatricals offered some distraction, but even these activities could be agonisingly repetitious. Dinner parties were arranged, but flying insects darting about around the badly cooked food made it unappetising. 'Everything is full of dust – books, dinner, clothes, everything.' Shoes had to be shaken in case a scorpion had curled up inside them, and insects gathered so thickly that every wine glass had to have a cover. All too frequently the humidity caused some people to drink too much alcohol and behave like idiots. The combination of these lonely ladies and dashing military men on leave from the strict discipline of army life gave the opportunity for a little discreet flirtation, which sometimes caused women to throw aside convention in their efforts to alleviate their boredom.

Yet the apparent shallowness and insufferable snobbery of the Anglo–Indian memsahibs, who they considered to be surrounded by an 'idle, dirty and stupid' native population, let nothing overlay a profound dedication to what they saw as their duty. They gamely stayed on in India with their menfolk despite the cruel climate, heartbreaking separation from their young ones, a desperate longing for home, and constant illness that could take their lives at any time. When the Indian Rebellion raged, this sense of duty, along with redoubtable courage and self-sacrifice, was evident time and again.

Chapter 5

The Rebellion Reaches Cawnpore

Just over 30 miles (50km) north of Cawnpore, in the town of Bithur, lived an influential local magnate called Dhondu Pant, the Maharajah of Bithur, who was more commonly known as Nana Sahib. He was the same Hindu caste as Lady Wheeler, and in General Wheeler's mistaken opinion he could be relied upon to support the British should the need arise. However, he was described as, 'A man of no capacity and debauched tastes … with strong passions, and no principles to guide them.'

He was born in 1824, to Narayan Bhatt and Ganga Bai, but on 7 June 1827 he was adopted by Baji Rao II, the last Peshwa (ruler) of the Maratha Empire, who had been dethroned by the British and settled in luxurious exile with the grant of a lavish £80,000 pension in exchange for his former dominions. Nana Sahib was well-educated and had married a daughter of the Chief of Sangli, but he could not speak much English. However, the British refused to grant a pension to the Nana Sahib on the death of his father on 28 January 1851 because he was not a son by blood.

His secretary was Azimullah Khan Yusufzai, who, on behalf of his master, was involved in a long drawn-out appeal to the East India Company and Lord Dalhousie's administration to restore the pension.

Azimullah was born in 1830, and he and his mother had been rescued from starvation during the famine of 1837–38, when they were provided shelter at a British charity school in Cawnpore. There he learnt English and French, which was a great achievement for an Indian in the nineteenth century. After working his way up from waiting on the tables of British officers to being appointed secretary to several officers, he became a trusted adviser to Nana Sahib.

Nana Sahib was allowed to inherit the savings of his adoptive father, which was still a considerable sum, part of which he used to send his shrewd and smooth-talking secretary to England in 1853 to plead his case with the few people who cared to listen. Azimullah was taken under the wing of Lucie, Lady Duff-Gordon, whose husband was a civil servant, and the cousin of the Prime Minister, Lord Aberdeen. He lodged with the Duff-Gordons at their home in Esher, where his charm, apparent good looks and gorgeous costumes prompted the assumption that he was a genuine Indian prince. This made him an attractive, exotic figure, and British ladies seem to have entered into compromising relationships with him. However, despite his social success, and the outlay of a massive sum of his master's money, the mission to London, including visits to East India House in Leadenhall Street, fell on deaf ears.

Azimullah returned to India bitter and frustrated, and on the way back he stopped to observe the British army in the Crimea. There he witnessed British soldiers starving and almost defeated. He did not witness any failings in the guts and determination of ordinary soldiers – that was impossible – but in administration and leadership, and with these visions of British failings he arrived in his homeland vowing to defeat who he then considered his enemies, and deviously planted in the Nana Sahib's mind the seeds of rebellion. Nana Sahib appointed him his dewan or prime minister, and referred to him as his 'Ambassador of Revolution'. He also brought back a French printing press, which was used to print and distribute subversive literature against the British Raj.

Nana Sahib financed his own body of troops, which included his adopted brother, Bala Rao, and his most notable field commander, Ramachandra Pandurang Tope, who is better known by his nickname Tantia Tope. He was born a Maratha Brahman sometime between 1814 and 1819, the only son of Pandurang Rao Tope and his wife Rukhmabai. He and Nana Sahib had been close friends since childhood, and he has been described as 'cruel and crafty'. One of his officers was Brigadier Jwala Prasad. When Nana Sahib was deprived of his father's pension in 1851, Tantia Tope, Jwala Prasad and the rebel leader Teeka Singh also became sworn enemies of the British. They knew they were not the only ones who were antagonised by the British, and conscious that 'The Devil's Wind' was in the air, they bided their time. These embittered men went to great pains to hide their resentment, and the Nana remained on the friendliest terms with General Wheeler and his Indian wife. Certainly, the general trusted him implicitly.

As the rising in Oudh gathered momentum, it was realised that the rebels in the province had few military leaders of quality. However, despite her divorce from the Nawab, the Begum of Oudh took charge of the affairs of the state of Oudh. She gained the respect of the rebels for agreeing to allow her ten-year-old son to become the ruler or Rani of Oudh, and appointed herself as his Regent. She supported fellow mutineers such as Nana Sahib, and with great sense of purpose she motivated the masses to rebel against the British. Such was her devotion and pledge to her people that she even went on to fortify the city of Lucknow in preparation for the fight against the advancing British troops. William Howard Russell of the *Times* noted in his diary: 'This Begum exhibits great energy and ability. She has excited all Oudh to take up the interests of her son, and the chiefs have sworn to be faithful to him.'

News of the outbreak of rebellion reached Cawnpore on 14 May, but it did not seem to have a great deal of effect on the sepoys or the civilian population at first. However, on 17 May Ann Fraser arrived in a bullet-riddled coach, and as curious people gathered around to inspect the holes made by sepoy bullets, she told of the revolt and subsequent bloodshed that was being carried out in Delhi.

Ann Fawcett Wray was born and baptised on 18 December 1829 at Cleasby, near Darlington in County Durham, but lived in the North Riding of Yorkshire. She was the daughter of Doctor Octavius Wray, who was born on 30 August 1793 at Town Head House in Thoralby, Yorkshire, and his wife, Sarah, the daughter of Christopher Wright and his wife, Jane (formerly Charge). Two paternal uncles had died while serving in the army. Lieutenant Thomas Fawcett Wray of the 7th Royal Fusiliers was killed in action during the storming of Badajoz in Spain in 1812, and Surgeon Christopher Wright Wray of the 87th Royal Irish Fusiliers was killed during an avalanche in Kashmir in 1853.

By mid-1831 they were in India, where Octavius was a surgeon with the 1st Bengal European Fusiliers. It is not clear if her mother was in India, but she was not involved in the events at Cawnpore and died at Catterick in Yorkshire on 15 April 1870. Octavius died of fever at Agra on 19 March 1836, leaving five children, the youngest, Thomas Charge being just two years old. Ann married Lieutenant George William Fraser of the 27th Bengal Native Infantry in Bengal on 28 November 1850. Lieutenant Fraser went missing in action at Oudh on 8 June 1857.

On arriving at work one day, Jonah Shepherd found the offices of the Commissariat and Ordnance Department alive with rumours and talk of bad tidings. 'Everybody in the station seemed to think that something dreadful was to occur, but were unable to see what it was.' Later that day a telegram arrived from Agra announcing that a large British force was to descend on Delhi to destroy the rebels, and announced that: 'The plague is stayed.' Many people gained relief from this, but those who could afford it still made preparations to leave in a hurry should the need arise.

A local lawyer named Nanak Chand, who would later relate many stories of his experiences in Cawnpore to George Trevelyan, had been troubled by the Nana's behaviour and did not trust him to the point where he reported his suspicions to the magistrate. However, the official rebuked him angrily as someone who had a grudge against the Nana.

On 16 May he went to visit a friend who was employed at the Treasury, when he overheard some of the officers of the guard 'uttering traitorous language', while allowing their men to argue with the townsfolk who were there on business, and generally make a nuisance of themselves. 'It began to be evident that nobody had any authority but the subadars and the sepoys.'

On 20 May all communication with Delhi and the outside world was cut off. That night a fire broke out in the lines of the 1st Native Infantry, which was suspected to have been started deliberately and caused concern that it might be the first sign of revolt, but it was found to have been accidental.

Each day new stories of the spread and ferocity of the rebellion came in, and rumours that the rebels were approaching Cawnpore sent deep concern through the cantonments. Several officers, including Colonel Lindsay, tried to persuade their families to go to Calcutta, but Kate wanted to stay with her son, so they remained. Fortunately, Major Lindsay's three sons were sent home to Rochester to stay with Mary Jane in the vicarage. Jonah Shepherd tried to persuade his family to escape to Allahabad but Ellen refused to leave without him.

One of the first incidents that showed bad karma in Cawnpore came when the Eurasian wife of the sergeant-major in the 53rd Native Infantry went shopping at the local market, where she was accosted by a sepoy wearing civilian clothes, who warned: 'You will none of you come here much oftener; you will not be alive another week.' As each day dawned with it came a growing sense of menace and distrust.

A breakdown of law and order among the Indian civilian population in Cawnpore was sure to follow. At first the British believed that nothing much would come of the disturbances other than a great amount of mischief and disorder, and in a letter of 15 May Emma Ewart stated that she knew that local villains known as goojurs, who had been notorious in the Cawnpore region for many years, were sure to take advantage of the situation. However, stories of horrifying events began to circulate among the cantonments.

General Wheeler still seems to have not been fully aware of the depth of discontent, because two days later he reported to the Government in Calcutta 'All well at Cawnpore. Quiet, but excitement continues among the people …' However, he still maintained his trust in the Nana, and even agreed that some of the women and children might be taken to Bithoor for their 'safety' if the situation worsened.

It is likely that Wheeler asked the Nana's advice on certain matters, and it is known that he received an assurance from the Nana that if the sepoys mutinied they would make for Delhi and leave the British in Cawnpore alone. The general invited the Nana to take over the magazine and the treasury with his household troops. The Nana willingly occupied these two main points – and waited!

On 3 June, only three days before the Cawnpore native troops rebelled, Wheeler sent Lieutenant O'Brien's company of about fifty men, including Ensign McGrath, further upland to Lucknow. Lieutenant O'Brien suffered a severe wound in the arm at Lucknow, but nothing like the suffering his fellow officer was to endure.

Mrs Maria Germon left a diary of her experiences at Lucknow during the siege, which stated:

Thursday, June 4th. While sitting in the garden, fifty Europeans of the 84th arrived in dawk carriages, Dr P and Major G with them.

Major G's regiment had mutinied, and they had with difficulty escaped with their lives. Dr P said they expected an attack between this (Lucknow) and Cawnpore, so as there were four soldiers to each carriage, two always kept watch outside with their muskets loaded, and the carriages were kept all together.

However, in a nine-page letter of 19 May, Kate Lindsay told her sister Mary back in Rochester of horrifying events in the area, including the death of her friend, Mrs Chalmers, who had been horribly murdered by a butcher: 'If our three native corps were to rise, which I pray to God to avert, we must all I am afraid perish.'

However, she was heartened to have been told that British troops were marching to the relief of Cawnpore, which: 'gave us a more cheering feeling, and we all went to church at half-past-six in the evening, and I think we all felt our minds sustained and comforted, and trusted that God would not quite forsake us.'

Martin Gubbins, who was the head of the Intelligence Department at Lucknow, had tried in vain to persuade Sir Henry Lawrence to send reinforcements to aid General Wheeler, and afterwards he tried to stop the general from entrusting the Nana Sahib in the protection of the treasury.

To disperse the Indian troops away from Cawnpore, and lessen the chances of a rebellion, General Wheeler decided to send them on various 'missions'. On 27 May he sent 240 troopers of the 2nd Oudh Irregulars to Fatehgarh, under the command of Captain Hayes, who had been acting as military secretary to Sir Henry Lawrence; and Lieutenant George Barbour, the adjutant of the 2nd Oudh Cavalry, to investigate the state of communications to the north. He was accompanied by General Thomas Carey of the 17th Bengal Native Infantry, and a volunteer named Richard Fayrer.

On the night of 31 May, Captain Hayes and General Carey departed to a nearby town to confer with the local magistrate, during which time the Indian troops rebelled and decapitated Mr Fayrer, and Lieutenant Barbour was killed as he tried to escape. When Hayes and Carey came back the next morning, unaware of the full situation, an older Indian officer galloped towards them and advised them to ride away. However, as the Indian officer was explaining the situation to them, the rebel Indian sowars raced towards them. Captain Hayes was cut down as he tried to ride away, while General Carey escaped to the relative safety of Agra.

Fletcher Fulton Compton Hayes was born in Calcutta on 9 January 1818, the only son of Commodore, Sir John Hayes, and his wife, Catherine. He was an Oxford graduate, appointed ensign in 1835, and served as assistant to Sleeman in the Thagi Department. At Maharajpur he was ADC to Sir Henry Gough.

George Douglas Barbour was born at Nasirabad in 1830 (his tombstone states 28 October 1829), the son of Captain G. A. Barbour of the 8th Bengal Light Cavalry. He was educated at Bath.

Richard Wilkinson Fayrer was born in Scotland in about 1835, the fifth of six sons in a family of eight children to Commander Robert John Fayrer RN, who was born at Heversham in Westmoreland (now Cumbria), on 11 March 1788, and his wife, Agnes (daughter of Richard Wilkinson, born 1800). While living in Heversham the family were friends with the poet William Wordsworth.

The 1841 census has them living at 4 Lower Mersey View in Everton, Walton-on-the-Hill in Liverpool. Robert Fayrer was away at sea, and Agnes was described as 'keeps lodgers', they having four living at the house at the time. On retiring from the navy, Robert Fayrer commanded steam boats from Liverpool to New York, and was thus a pioneer of ocean steam navigation. The 1851 census has them living at Warmley Lodge at St Saviour on the island of Jersey. Richard became a cadet in the Australian Mounted Police, and was: 'a young man of great promise'.

Among mounting tension, Colonel Ewart tried his best to avert the crisis by continuing to stay with his men as much as he could, and even sleep among them out in the barracks to show his trust.

Emma Ewart wrote to her sister, Fanny, and reflected on how much risk her husband was taking by continuing to go out among his men. She said he 'flinched not an instant in the performance of his duty', preferring to stay with his regiment whatever happened. This was particularly impressive because Emma states that sepoys had been overheard discussing 'the destruction of the officers'. However, she knew that the Karma was very bad, and she wrote later 'We want a Napier now …' The reason for such a wish is explained in Chapter 10.

Chapter 6

Fatehgarh Fugitives

The military presence in the cantonment town of Fatehgarh consisted of the 10th Bengal Native Infantry. The Indian NCOs of this regiment stated that they would not murder their officers, but they added that if another regiment was to do so 'it was not their fault'. They made this promise knowing that the 2nd Oudh Irregulars were approaching the city and the 41st Bengal Native Infantry had mutinied at nearby Seetapore and had committed many murders. Included in the victims was Henry Bensley Thornhill, his wife, Emily Heathfield, their infant daughter Catherine, and their nurse, who had been murderously shot down by the mutineers. When some of the 2nd Oudh Irregulars arrived in the city the 10th Native Infantry began to fraternise with them, and when the 41st arrived the city rose up in revolt, thus rendering the place untenable, and the situation became extremely dangerous.

The Nawab of Furruckabad was said to be acting with great fanaticism and cruelty, and the mutineers began to murder the Europeans. A native Christian and other sources reported that an indigo printer named Mr Bridges, his wife, his mother-in-law Mrs Defontaine, and their daughter, Mrs Eckford, were all blown from guns at Fatehgarh. This hideous type of execution was used by both sides in the conflict. The victim was strapped across the muzzle of a big gun and fired with a flash and a roar. Above the smoke, legs, arms and heads flew in all directions, followed by an obscene shower of gore that covered the observers. It was practised so often that one man stated: 'Such is the force of habit we now think little of it.'

The Fatehgarh fort was bravely defended for nine days, with few guns and little ammunition. Lieutenant-Colonel Thomas Tudor Tucker of the 8th Bengal Light Cavalry was among the slain. He had taken a shot through a loophole, and as he exposed himself at the loophole to check the effect, he was shot dead. He left his large family of Louisa Isabella,

Annie, Louisa, George, and two children described only as Miss Tucker and 'L'.

The fort was evacuated on 3 June, and to try to save themselves about 140 Europeans left the town in boats under cover of darkness at two o'clock on the morning of 4 June. The boats came under heavy fire at Khoosumkhor, and later about forty went to seek refuge at the fort of Hardeo Bakhsh at Dharampur, and the rest went on down the river. However, they were fired upon by mutineers on both banks of the river, and many were killed or wounded. One of the boats became unmanageable, they had to mend the rudder of another, and the third craft got stuck on a muddy bank near the Nana's palace at Bithoor. As they were trying to free it they were attacked by mutineers. Several took to the water and drowned, or were hacked to death or shot.

Robert Lowis was one of the men who were drowned near Bithur during an attack on his boat, and Doctor Maltby was seriously wounded. After the boat was captured, a native Indian nursemaid named Nancy Lang refused to give up a baby in her care to the rebels, so she and the baby were murdered. Later court evidence stated: 'There was one doctor, with wife and child a few days old; the brutes floated off the child on the Ganges on a plank from the boat between Bithur and Cawnpore.' All the survivors were captured and taken to Cawnpore.

Colonel George Acklom Smith of the 10th Bengal Native Infantry was born in 1815, the only child of the Reverend Richard Smith and his wife, Mary (formerly Acklom). Robert Bensley Thornhill was a judge at Farruckpur. He had his wife, Mary, and children, Charles Cudbert and Mary Catherine, with him.

Colonel Andrew Goldie of the 46th Bengal Native Infantry was born on 21 March 1794, in the village of Athelstaneford, east of Edinburgh, the son of the Reverend George Goldie (1748–1804), Presbyterian minister of St Andrew's Church from 1778 to 1804, and his second wife, Magdalene Howden (1752–1836). Reverend Goldie had four children from his first marriage and Andrew was one of ten children from his second marriage. He entered the 46th Bengal Native Infantry, and became military auditor general at Cawnpore.

Andrew married a Eurasian woman named Meerium Khanum, whose name was anglicised to Mary Graham, who had died before 1857, and they had nine children. One of his daughters, Alice, died in 1856, and with him at Cawnpore were Mary, his eldest daughter of seven, who was born on 18 December 1820, and his fifth daughter, Emily, who was born on 28 December 1827. His two youngest children were both boys; James was a colonel in the Indian Army, and Alexander was a doctor in Edinburgh. Alexander had been born in India in 1842, and baptised at Tonbridge in Kent on 11 October 1843. They were both educated at Walthamstow House School.

Robert Bensley Thornhill was born in 1818 and baptised on 12 July 1818 at St John the Evangelist, Great Stanmore in Middlesex. He was the son of the late John Thornhill (1773–1841), a director of the East India Company, and his wife Henriette Philippine (formerly Beaufoy) (1785–1866). The family home was at Liston Hall near Long Melford in Suffolk. Robert was educated at Haileybury, 1835–36. In 1839 he married Mary White Siddons (born in 1821). They had six boys and a girl in the 1840s. One of them, Edward Augustus, was born in Oxfordshire on 2 October 1848. They had two children at Cawnpore named Charles Cudbert, aged five, and Mary Catherine, who had been born at West Bengal on 5 March 1855.

Robert Nisbet Lowis was born in 1831 at St Ninians in Stirling, Scotland, and he was baptised there on 25 August 1831. He was the son of John Lowis (born 19 January 1801), who was a member of the supreme court of India, and his wife, Louisa (formally Fendall), a daughter of the governor of Singapore. Robert was educated at Bath, and Haileybury from 1849 to 1851, arriving in India in 1851, where he was appointed joint magistrate at Moradabad.

Robert had married Emma McCausland, who was of Irish descent, but had been born on 16 August 1837 at Subatoo in India, one of seven children to Lieutenant-General John Kennedy McCausland of the 70th Bengal Native Infantry, and his wife, Emma, the daughter of Colonel William Conrad Faithfull, and his wife Maria (formerly Agg). At Fatehgarh they had two girls, Eliza and Emma Maria, the latter being born at Fatehgarh in 1855, and another child.

Samuel Maltby was born at the rectory in the village of Shelton, near Newark-on-Trent, and he was baptised on 29 September 1820. He was the oldest child of the Reverend John Ince Maltby and his wife, Elizabeth (formerly Weston). His uncle, Samuel Maltby, was a colonel with the East India Company. In 1841 he was a dresser, or house surgeon, at St Thomas's Hospital in Southwark, London. He qualified as a surgeon in 1842, and was probably introduced into the service of the East India Company by his uncle. He married Anne (born 1812), the only daughter of Lieutenant-General G. W. E. Lloyd CB, on 11 August 1852, at Agra in West Bengal.

Doctor Maltby retired from service with the East India Company soon after their marriage, and at the time of the outbreak he was giving medical aid to troops at the garrison. Anne was with him, and she is believed to have been pregnant with their first child.

Chapter 7

The Fort of Despair

Mainly to protect the civilians, General Wheeler decided to give them a place of refuge. One of two possible strong points was the magazine, which contained large stocks of weapons and ammunition. It was close by the river and therefore could provide a good getaway in an emergency. The other consisted of two barrack buildings situated in the open, well away from the river near the main road. The barracks were chosen, and Wheeler, probably with some input from Lieutenant Jervis, detailed some men to build an entrenchment of loose earth around it. It was only 4ft high and totally inadequate, and the disadvantages of the position should have been obvious to an experienced soldier. It is likely that Wheeler chose this position because he thought that reinforcements would come up the road from the south at Allahabad.

Lieutenant Daniell had been a favourite of the Nana at his palace in Bithoor, so much so that on one occasion he took a diamond ring off his finger and gave it to the British officer as a gift. Soon after the entrenchment had been constructed he met Azimullah, who pointed at the position and sneered mockingly: 'What do you call that place you are making out in the plain?' and suggested it should be named the fort of despair. 'No,' said Daniell, 'we shall call it the fort of victory!' To which Azimullah just laughed.

Mrs Germon stated:

Friday, 16 October. General Wheeler did not make the entrenchment at the magazine, because he had no idea that there was any ammunition in it; he thought it was filled with old tents, &c., whereas a great portion of the ammunition brought against us came from there, besides what was expended by the enemy at Cawnpore. This seems hardly credible in a General of Division, but I believe it is correct.

On 21 May General Wheeler ordered some wagons to go out and collect all the arms and accoutrements they could find, and he gave orders to bring twenty-five days' supplies into the entrenchment, with peas and flour forming the bulk of the food obtained. Later that day, General Wheeler and Captain Moore got all the people together, including the women and children, and told them what their duties would be during the siege. After that he told them to go and bring in all the furniture, boxes and bedding they could, and these items were scattered all around the defences with the intention of hindering any enemy cavalry charges. He got them to construct gun-emplacements, which were no more than gaps in the defences. They placed the guns in the gaps – and prepared for the worst.

Colonel Larkins was in overall command of the artillery. One gun was placed to the north of the entrenchment in the charge of Captains Vibart and Jenkins. This position was called The Redan, because it was an earthwork that jutted out from the main line of the defences and therefore protected the whole of the area to the north, including the flanks. To their right, or the north-east, was Lieutenant St George Ashe of the artillery (Thomson lists him as with the Oudh Irregular Cavalry), with the twenty-four-pounder howitzer he had brought from Lucknow on 26 May, and two nine-pounders; assisted by Lieutenant Sotheby. The north-west was protected by a gun under the command of Lieutenant Francis Whiting of the Bengal Engineers, assisted by Lieutenant Jervis, and this was protected to the front by three lines of pits known as *trous de loup*, designed to prevent cavalry charges by the rebels. The west section of the barricade was defended by three nine-pounders under Captain Dempster and Lieutenant John Nickleson Martin of the artillery. Flanking the west battery in support they placed a smaller rifled three-pounder, with a detachment under the command of Major Walter Roger Prout of the 56th Bengal Native Infantry. The main guard from south to west was in the charge of Captain Adam Montague Turnbull (Mowbray states he was a lieutenant) of the 13th Bengal Native Infantry; 2nd Lieutenants James Alexander Haldane Eckford and F. W. Burney of the artillery, assisted by Lieutenant de la Fosse, had charge of the south-east battery, with three nine-pounders; and Captain George Kempland of the 56th Bengal Native Infantry was posted on the south side.

There was an area to the west of the entrenchment that was virtually a building site, where there were a number of red-brick barrack buildings all about 200 paces in length, intended to be two-storeys high, but they were in various stages of construction and no floors had been finished. Most were about 7ft high, except numbers 2 and 3, which were 40ft high. They ran diagonally, with Barracks number 1 being furthest north-west, Barracks 4 was the only one with a roof, and there was a deep well attached to Barracks 5, which was closest to the south-west entrenchment wall across from the main guard. They commanded the British positions in the entrenchment and therefore some of them had to be defended so they could not be taken over by the rebels. For reasons of hygiene and to ward off disease it was decided early on to put the bodies of the dead in this sepulchre well.

As the day progressed people began to enter the entrenchment, and at midday Wheeler ordered that a gun should be fired to warn all the other inhabitants that they should make their way there to relative safety. Not long afterwards, people began to appear: 'flocking from all directions'.

Jonah Shepherd saw the panic that had taken over many of his colleagues and other people at the Commissariat, so he sent a note to his friend, John Hay, to try to get some information. Hay replied that he was fleeing to the entrenchment, and urgently advised Jonah to do the same. Jonah collected his confused and by that time panic-stricken family and rushed them off to the entrenchment. He remembered later: 'On our way we met several of our acquaintances going in the same direction who wished to know the cause of the sudden flight.' However, nobody actually knew for sure! He shook his head in trepidation at what he saw in the fort, as he arrived as one of the last families to enter.

Emma Ewart described the scene in her first letter of three that have been preserved:

Oh! Such a scene dear Fanny. Men, officers, women and children, beds and chairs all mingled together inside and out of the barracks, some talking and even laughing, some very frightened, some defiant, others despairing. Those guns in front of our position and then behind a trench in course of foundation all round – such sickening sights these peaceful women, and then the miserable reflection that all this ghastly show is caused not by open foes, but by the treachery of those we have fed and pampered and honoured and trusted in for so many years – Oh! I cannot dwell upon the harrowing thoughts.

On his arrival at Cawnpore, Captain Fletcher Hayes had witnessed:

> … a frightful scene of confusion, fright and bad arrangement. People of all kinds, of every colour, sect and profession were crowding into the barracks. I saw quite enough to convince me that if any insurrection takes place we shall have no-one to thank but ourselves, because we have now shown the natives how very easily we can become frightened, and when frightened utterly helpless.

Later in the year, Lady Inglis wrote:

> I went to see the entrenchments, or rather the ruined barracks, in which our poor countrymen and women maintained so noble a struggle. I could not have believed that any human beings could have stood out for one day in such a place. The walls inside and out were riddled with shot: you could hardly put your hand on a clear spot. The ditch and wall – it is absurd to call it a fortification – any child could have jumped over; and yet behind these for three weeks the little force held their own against overwhelming numbers of the enemy, who had not the courage to approach them. As I looked, I thought how small were the troubles and trials of Lucknow in comparison. The agony and miseries these poor creatures must have suffered defies even imagination to conceive; they must have, as it were, died daily. Doubtless, if the truth could be recorded, many a noble deed of heroism and self-denial was enacted here …

'Alarming reports continued to fly about the station daily', and Jonah Shepherd had absolutely no confidence that the entrenchment was strong enough to protect his family. He was thinking of ways to get away from it almost as soon as he had entered. He rented two bungalows in a native contractor's name, and intended to seek refuge there as a family of local Indians if the situation became desperate. He even got his wife and sister to make disguises based on the Ayah's clothing. However, at the back of his mind he knew that their fair skin was likely to give their identity away to the sepoys.

On 25 May Lieutenant Angelo took his family into the entrenchment, but he was very suspicious of the situation. His wife, Helena, stated 'This entrenched camp is a singular scene – parties of officers and ladies singing and laughing in one place – gentlemen assembled in the open air – all noise and bustle and one would imagine it some gay assembly.'

Fred became attached to a gun battery, but Helena noticed he had serious doubts in his mind, and eventually he insisted that his family should accompany a Mrs Volk to Calcutta, and they left on the evening of 28 May. Helena was not happy about separating from her husband, but they were probably the last people who left Cawnpore for safety before the outbreak, and his insistence saved their lives.

Louisa Chalwin recorded that her husband had vowed that 'he would thankfully send me home now, if it could be easily done'. However, she believed that things had died down a bit, security might soon be re-established, and she hoped 'that there may be no need for such precautions'. However, it only proved to be the calm before the storm.

On 31 May, Colonel Ewart wrote to friends in England:

I do not wish to write gloomily, but there is no use disguising the facts that we are in the utmost danger, and, as I have said, if the troops do mutiny my life must almost certainly be sacrificed. But I do not think they will venture to attack the entrenched position that is held by the European troops. So I hope in God that Emma and my child will be saved.

The Hillersdens and their two children have been staying with us since the 21st, when the danger became imminent, as it was no longer safe for them to remain in their own house four miles from the cantonments.

And now dear A___ farewell. If under God's providence this be the last time I am to write to you, I entreat you to forgive all I have ever done to trouble you, and to think kindly of me. I know you will be everything a mother can be to my boy. I cannot write to him this time, dear little fellow; kiss him for me; kind love to M___ and my brothers.

Emma Ewart stated:

> For ourselves I need only say, that even if our position should be
> strong enough to hold out, there is the dreadful exposure to the heat
> of May and June, together with the privations and confinement of
> besieged sufferers, to render it very unlikely that we can survive the
> disasters which may fall upon us any day, and hour. I am going to
> despatch this to Calcutta, to be sent through our agents there, that
> you may know our situation.
>
> My dear little child is looking very delicate. My prayer is that
> she [baby] may be spared much suffering – the bitterness of death
> has been tasted by us many, many times during the last fortnight.
> Should the reality come I hope we may find strength to meet it with
> a truly Christian courage. It is not hard to die oneself but to see a
> dear child suffer and perish, that is the hard, the bitter trial, the cup
> which I must drink should God not deem it fit that it pass from me.
>
> My companion, Mrs Hillersdon is delightful. Poor young thing!
> She has such a gentle spirit, so unmurmuring, so desirous to meet
> the trial rightly, so unselfish and sweet in every way. Her husband
> is an excellent man, and of course very much exposed to danger,
> almost as much as mine. She has two children, and we feel that our
> duty to our little ones demands that we should exert ourselves to
> keep up health and spirits as much as possible.
>
> There is a reverse to this sad picture. Delhi may be re-taken in a
> short time, aid may come to us, and all may subside into tranquillity
> once more. Let us hope for the best, do our duty, and trust in God
> above all things. Should I be spared I will write to you by the latest
> date. We must not give way to despondency for at the worst we know
> we are in God's hands and He does not for an instant forsake us. He
> will be with us in the valley of the shadow of death also and we need
> fear no evil. God bless you.
>
> Our weak position here, with a mere handful of Europeans, places
> us in very great danger; and daily and hourly we are looking for
> disasters. It is supposed that the commandants here have shown
> wonderful tact, and that their measure of boldly facing the danger
> by going out to sleep amongst their men, has had a wonderful effect

on restraining them. But everybody knows that this cannot last. Any accidental spark may set the whole of the regiments of infantry, and one of cavalry, in a blaze of mutiny; and even if we keep our position where we are entrenched, with six guns, officers must be sacrificed; and I do not attempt to conceal from myself that my husband runs greater risk than any one of the whole force. Europeans are almost daily arriving from Calcutta, but in small numbers, twenty or thirty at a time. Every day that we escape free of disturbance adds to our strength, and gives a better chance for our lives. Property is not to be thought of, as conflagrations always accompany the outbreaks, and we may be quite sure of our bungalows being burnt down directly troubles commence.

Such nights of anxiety I would never have believed possible, and the days are full of excitement. Every note and every message come pregnant with events and alarms. Another fortnight, we expect, will decide our fate, and, whatever it may be, I trust we shall be enabled to bear it. If these are my last words to you dearest Fanny you will remember them lovingly and always bear in mind that your affection and the love we have had for each other is an ingredient of comfort in these biter times.

The last telegraph from Cawnpore that reached its destination before the lines were cut was sent by General Wheeler on 3 June to the secretary of the Government of India in Calcutta:

All the orders and proclamations have been sent express as the telegraph communication between this and Agra is obstructed.

Sir Henry Lawrence having expressed some uneasiness, I have just sent him by post carriages out of my small force two officers and fifty men of Her Majesty's 84th Foot; conveyance for more not available. This leaves me weak, but I trust to holding my own until more Europeans arrive.

Finally, on 4 June, the 2nd Light Cavalry broke out in open revolt and set fire to the riding master's bungalow as a show of defiance. The 1st Native Infantry broke out from their parade ground later that day, and the 56th

Native Infantry mutinied on the following morning. The 53rd Native Infantry refused to join the other units at first and remained in their lines, apparently cooking their dinners. However, for some unknown misunderstanding, Lieutenant Ashe's battery at the north-east of the entrenchment opened up on them and they were driven out by the nine-pounder shells.

As Private Murphy stood on sentry duty at the main entrance, about 100 sepoys approached him and said that they wanted to leave – forcefully if necessary. Murphy stood his ground and told them that he could allow people to come in but his orders were not to let anyone out. Murphy realised that they were not going to accept his words so he let off a few warning shots determined to carry out his orders. It was a tense situation, but General Wheeler and some other officers intervened and told Murphy to allow them to pass. All the horses belonging to the British were tied outside the fort, so the rebels stole them and took them into the enemy lines.

At first the mutineers made their way towards Delhi, but they were eventually persuaded by the Nana and Azimullah to return to Cawnpore and attack the Europeans. On 6 June, the rebels showed complete lack of knowledge concerning military tactics when they gave away the element of surprise and General Wheeler received a warning from the Nana that the entrenchment would soon be attacked. On Sunday morning, 7 June, they heard the sounds of rebel forces approaching from the north, and saw their green standards waving in the distance, so Lieutenant Ashe took out a large party of volunteers and his guns to reconnoitre the area. After going out about 500 paces they caught full sight of the dense masses of the sepoy army and fell back into the entrenchment. Unfortunately, Ashe's old schoolmate, Lieutenant Ashburner, lost control of his horse and it bolted into the midst of the sepoys, who attacked him and killed him. A railway worker named Murphy was also injured, to such an extent that he did not see the day out before he died. A coffin was found in a corner of the hospital, and he was the only person to be buried in such a way.

And so, while church bells were ringing in England calling congregations to church for morning service, all the officers were called into the entrenchment, and soon the fort was surrounded by the rebels.

At ten o'clock in the morning the first cannonball from an enemy nine-pounder gun was fired at the entrenchment. It bounded towards its target, hit the top of the mud wall, glided over it, and broke the leg of a native footman standing near the tile-roofed barrack building. Great screams of fright rang out from within the building from the women and children. All the defenders were ordered to take their posts under fire for the first time.

It soon became apparent that they were under siege, and Amy Horne described the scene as she saw it:

> The opening day of the siege was one of the most terrible sights which our eyes now beheld; the whole surrounding country seemed covered with men at arms, on horse and on foot, and they presented a most formidable appearance. They seemed such odds to keep at bay from out Lilliputian defences.
>
> The site of our entrenchment was surrounded by large and substantial buildings … occupied by the rebels, and from roof and window, all day, a shower of bullets poured down on us in our exposed positions. Shell likewise kept falling all over the entrenchment … one shell killed seven women as it fell hissing into the trenches and burst. Windows and doors were soon shot off their sockets, and the shot and shell began to play freely through the denuded buildings …

Despite the obvious dangers, some people had chosen to stay in the town. However, the Nana had many of them hunted down and either murdered or taken hostage. On 8 June, he sent a party of mercenaries to the residence of Edward Greenway, who was giving shelter to Captain William Charles Hollings, an officer recently cashiered by court martial. He bravely helped the Greenway family to defend themselves for two days, until his last cartridge had been expended, then he walked out onto an upper balcony of the house with his arms raised above his head and shouted to the attackers to take his life. A sniper hidden in a tree sent a bullet through his heart. Then they secured Edward, his wife, his sister, and his children, and took them as prisoners to the Nana; who ordered them into confinement at his headquarters in the Savada House, with the expectation of obtaining a ransom, although it was said that he intended to kill them whether a ransom was paid or not. Mrs Charles Greenway, the mother of Samuel Greenway, was considered too old to go into the entrenchment. She was not murdered but 'received much annoyance from the rebels'. Mary Ann, an Ayah to Mrs Greenway, is believed to have escaped on 27 June and remained hidden in the city.

A watchmaker and jeweller, Henry Jacobi, was in the entrenchment when his wife, Emma, and three children, Henry, Hugh and Lucy were also taken into captivity in the house. She was the daughter of a Bengal artilleryman serving in India. They also had a grown-up son named William, whose wife, Isabella remained in the city and survived. His brother, Frederick Ernest, and his wife, Sophia Matilda, were also in the entrenchment. Fortunately for them they had sent their twelve-year-old daughter, Charlotte Maria, to Calcutta for health reasons.

On about the same day, Lady Inglis, who was in a similar situation at Lucknow, wrote in her diary:

> News arrived from Cawnpore describing the garrison there as being in great distress. We felt deeply anxious about them. There were three officers in Lucknow whose wives were in Cawnpore. One, Captain Evans, was in our house, and his wretched face used quite to haunt me. He seldom spoke.
>
> Mowbray Thomson stated: 'My friend Major Evans had to endure the most intense solitude for his beloved wife, while he was engaged in the defence of Lucknow.'
>
> Unfortunately, the guns and gunners were mostly unprotected from the murderous fire from the enemy and they suffered badly. In support of the batteries, infantry was posted about fifteen paces apart, and under the precarious cover of the low mud wall, and in some cases they had to be relieved by non-combatants. Each man had several muskets close by with bayonets fixed in case of any attempted rush upon them by the enemy. Not very long after placing his men and guns in their positions, Colonel Larkins became so overcome with exhaustion and the effects of the heat that he was forced to stand down from his duties.

Not surprisingly, the first casualty within the entrenchment was a gunner, named Patrick McGuire, who was helping to man the gun under the command of Captain Dempster to the west of the defences opposite the barrack buildings that had been taken over by the rebels. A round shot came bounding towards the battery, and several men, including McGuire saw it coming. However, he seems to have become transfixed by it, like a cat in the beam of a headlight, and he failed to get out of the way in time before it thumped into him and killed him. The men were too busy to remove his body, so they simply threw a blanket over him and left him where he fell until nightfall, when he could be removed under the cover of darkness. Amy Horne stated that another artillery officer:

> had just come into the barracks from the trenches, and had taken a seat in the veranda to rest himself. He hadn't sat down for more than a minute when a shot struck him full in the face, taking his head clean off. His body continued to remain seated, his hands falling by his sides, the blood gushing from between his shoulders like a fountain, and falling on those who rushed to his rescue.

On 9 June, Emma Larkins, who had three young children with her, wrote to her four children back in England what is believed to be the last letter to get out of Cawnpore. In it she shows the terrible feelings of hopelessness and despair being suffered by the garrison, and how most of them turned to their God for solace:

> I write this, dearest Henrietta, in the belief that our hour of departure is come. The whole of the troops rose here and we took refuge in a barrack. We are hemmed in by overpowering numbers that there seems no hope of escape. Only about 40 Europeans are left of 120 men; a sad number to hold out against an overpowering enemy. Many joined the cavalry and infantry, and they have six guns against us. The walls are going. This is an awful hour, my darling Henrietta. Jessie, Emily and Georgie [her children] cling to us. Dearest George [her husband] has been well up to today, but he is, I grieve to say, now obliged to abandon his post. This is to my grief. Many brave men have fallen today. The siege has lasted four days!
>
> Oh, let this be a warning to your government never again to place British officers and men in such a pitiful position; only 120

European soldiers in Cawnpore! It is sad and painful to reflect on that our lives are to be sacrificed in such a condition.

Give my love to my sweet girls. Tell them that there is but one thing needful: Tell them to seek sorrowing that faith sure and steadfast, an anchor of the soul. Connie, darling, your mamma has longed to see and know you. [she had been left behind in England at the age of three and a half years] Seek your God and Heaven in spirit. Alice, my sweet child, remember your creator in the days of your youth, seek him till you can say: 'I have found him!' Ellen, my little lamb, I must not see you again in the flesh, but remember I will look for you where sorrow and disappointment can never enter. Harry, dear boy, my heart yearns over you. Oh, dear boy, if you saw the position your little brother and sisters are in you would weep over ever having pleased your own desires. Seek your God and heaven, and serve and please him, and always hate whatever is sinful. Dearest Henrietta, we leave them all in the hands of God and your tender watching.

My dear love to all my dear friends, Peace dearest Henrietta, which passes knowledge be with you; my gratitude to you is unchanged. *[written on the outside of the envelop it stated]:* I have given this to nun-nah, who hopes to escape and …

It seems she became too distressed to write clearly after that because the rest is indistinguishable.

The month of June is one of the warmest of the season and the sun was at its hottest. Gun barrels burned the hand that held them, and there was little or no protection from the scorching heat. Captain Thomson estimated the temperatures to range between 120 and 138 degrees Fahrenheit.

About sixty years later a large underground room was discovered below the barracks that would have given cool shade from the heat and protection from the rebel bullets and heavy artillery, but those in the entrenchment were unaware of its existence.

Many years later, General George MacMunn of the Royal Artillery stated 'In the 1920s it was found that one of the two barracks has an underground chamber, capable of sheltering many, which was unknown to the garrison.'

However, according to Andrew Ward it was in a position where people may have become trapped inside when the thatched barrack was set on fire. Apparently, it can still be seen to this day, but it is snake-infested.

There was only one well within the entrenchment that had to supply all of the defenders, but as the fire from the enemy became more intense it was almost impossible to get there and back without being killed. The only real chance they had of obtaining any water was in the very early hours of the morning under cover of darkness. 'It became quite impossible to obtain a bag of water even for 10 or 15 rupees.'

Despite the hardship, most of the men remained in good spirits because they expected to be relieved soon. However, as each day passed and no relief came the situation became more desperate and the defenders were 'Falling off like flies because of want of food.'

In his capacity as head of the commissariat, Captain Williamson worked hard to try to provide sustenance for the besieged. Captain Thomson stated:

> It was owing to the indefatigable exertions of this estimable man that any food at all was brought into the entrenchment. Before the commencement of the siege, and even after the cantonment had fallen into the possession of the rebels, Captain Williamson went out with a party of volunteers, and brought in some barrels of rum and beer.

Later he superintended the giving out of provisions, which were distributed equally regardless of rank. After a while stray dogs and a bullock were killed to make into soup as part of the staple diet, and eventually when it became possible to shoot down a sowar of the enemy cavalry it was more to capture the horse for the soup ration than to kill the man on it.

Lieutenant Thomson told of an incident when a bull came grazing nearby and was shot down. However, it was lying dead about 300 paces away and any attempt to retrieve it would put them in great peril from the enemy watching all around. Nevertheless, Captain Moore got some rope and with a number of men he moved out of the entrenchment. They came under fire as some of them tied the beast by the back legs and the horns, and with cheers of encouragement from the mud walls they dragged it back to the entrenchment. They received casualties but none of the wounds proved fatal. The bull was made into a beefy soup, and from then onwards any horse or dog that came anywhere near the barricades suffered the same fate.

Soon after the siege began Lieutenant Saunders was wounded in the left breast by grapeshot. Nevertheless, he continued to take an active part in the defence of the entrenchment and quickly emerged as one of Wheeler's most unyielding and determined officers.

Having stress levels constantly high, coupled with suffering the dreadful heat and weakened by hunger, diseases such as smallpox and cholera were rife. The fatal symptoms were firstly headache and drowsiness, followed by vomiting and gradual insensibility, which terminated in death. The number of victims grew each day. A lady named Mrs Wade was the first to succumb to fever, and she was the only civilian buried inside the entrenchment.

Lieutenant Redman had written home to his family stating he was grateful that 'he had no wife with him to share the surpassing horrors of the situation'.

On the morning of 10 June a horseman was seen galloping hell-for-leather towards the entrenchment. Some of the pickets raised their weapons and at least one fired and wounded the advancing horse, but it reeled and stayed on its legs, and as the rider got close enough to be recognised as a British army officer, a call rang out 'hold your fire!' The horse leapt over the parapet and was brought to a halt, and the rider dismounted '… in a most distressed and exhausted condition'.

It was Lieutenant Augustus Joseph Boulton of the 7th Bengal Native Cavalry. He had been sent out from Lucknow with the 48th Native Infantry and some sowars of his own regiment to keep some of the roads free from rebels, but the two Indian units had mutinied. His four fellow officers were all murdered in a most brutal way, and Lieutenant Boulton had received a bullet in the cheek that had shattered some of his teeth as he rode away. He was chased by a party of sowars for several miles, but after jumping a wide ditch he managed to get away from them on the outskirts of Nowabgunj. He had spent a restless night out on the plains close to the Nana Sahib's men before riding to the precarious salvation of the entrenchment. Lieutenant Thomson stated: 'He joined the outpicket under Captain Jenkins, and although a great sufferer from the wound in his cheek, he proved a valuable addition to our strength.'

As Major Lindsay lay on his bed in the barracks on 17 June, an enemy round shot smashed into the other side of the wall, sending a spray of masonry splinters into the room. The major screamed out in pain and shock and threw his hands to his face as he caught the main force of the blast. When Kate pulled his hands away they saw that his eyes were dreadfully cut and 'had turned to a pulp'. He could not see, and he riled in agony from the unbearable pain. Lily was already weak with fever, and the shock of seeing her husband in such dire straits was too much for her to bear and she succumbed later that day. William was put out of his misery soon after his wife.

Doctor Newenham helped to tend to the wounded and sick until he became ill himself and died of fever. His death was followed by that of Charlotte and then Isabella. Captain Turner's wife, Ellen, and Louise Chalwin became victims, as did the Greenway daughters, Ann and Rosaline, and an infant child, followed by Thomas and Louisa. Captain Halliday's daughter, Emma Mabel, died of fever, and his wife Emma was suffering from smallpox. To try to help her gain some strength he had collected two lots of horse soup and they were eating it together when he was struck by a cannonball. Colonel Ewart and his wife, Emma, had to suffer 'the hard and bitter trial' of their 'very delicate' little daughter, Agnes Emma, as she died of heatstroke and shock.

The list of dreadful incidents and deaths grew more and more each day. According to Captain Thomson, the following incidents happened in the space of one hour. Lieutenant William Prole of the 53rd Native Infantry was at the main guard talking to his unit's adjutant, Lieutenant Herbert Armstrong, who was unwell. He was struck by a musket ball and fell to the ground. Captain Thomson came to his assistance, lifted him up, and by throwing one arm across his shoulders and putting his own arm around the injured man's waist he was able to help him to hobble to the barracks to get medical attention from the doctors. As he was doing so a ball hit him under his right shoulder blade, and the two men fell to the ground in a pile. Gilbert Bax of the 48th Native Infantry had come to assist them both when a bullet pierced his shoulder blade, causing a serious wound that eventually proved fatal. Some sources state that he was killed during a sortie to Seetapore on 3 June.

Lieutenant-Colonel Williams was wounded early in the siege, and heatstroke further reduced his constitution until he died on 8 June, with his wife and three daughters at his side. Their daughter, Mary, died soon afterwards, apparently having been frightened to death by the constant explosions. The grieving mother, Mary, received a disfiguring bullet wound to her upper lip, and Georgina received a bullet wound right through her shoulder blade. Only Fanny seems to have remained unscathed.

Lydia Hillersdon had been taken into the tile-roofed barracks to give birth, which she did during the first week of the siege. While she was recovering, her husband Charles wanted to have a private conversation with her and they went outside to an area that they thought was out of view from the enemy batteries, near the verandah of the tile-roofed barrack close to the soldiers' garden. Unfortunately, he was unaware that the enemy had set up a new battery, and he was exposed to the aim of the rebel gunners. Lydia was suddenly faced with the heartbreaking spectacle of seeing a cannonball thump into his stomach and quite literally smash him to pieces. Two days later she was standing in about the same place when another ball smashed into the verandah nearby and she was buried in a heap of heavy rubble. Several people ran to her aid and managed to pull her clear, but she had received severe head injuries and she died soon afterwards 'In great distress'. She was buried at the edge of the soldiers' garden.

What was described as an 'appalling spectacle' followed. While manning his post at the entrenchment wall, Lieutenant Wheeler was wounded and had to retire to the tile-roofed barrack to be nursed by his family. All the doors had been blown off the building and offered no protection. He collapsed on the sofa, and as either Eliza or Ulrica was fanning him to try to bring him round, a cannonball came through the room and took off his head, right in front of his poor father and mother, and two sisters. It is impossible to imagine how these poor people felt afterwards.

On 10 June seven soldiers' wives were sitting together in Lieutenant Whiting's battery to the north-west of the defences when an enemy mortar shell fell among them and the fierce explosion killed and wounded

A water colour of a street scene at Cawnpore, showing the main thoroughfare known as the Chouk, with narrow streets leading off it to bazaars and markets. The picture was produced by Seeta Ram in about 1815.

Sir Hugh Wheeler was one of the most experienced and popular officers in the East India Company's service. However, he was in his seventies and in ill-health when he took command of the Cawnpore garrison at the time of the outbreak, and no amount of experience could have prepared him for the challenges he had to face.

Unlike rebel leaders who were true to the cause, such as Tantia Tope, the Rani Laxmibai of Jhansi, and the Begum Hazrad Mahal of Oudh, it is debatable if the – 'miscreant' – the Nana Sahib disliked the British because of a desire for Indian independence or simply financial gain.

Azimullah Khan Yusufzai was Nana Sahib's secretary. Having been rebuffed by the authorities in London he returned to India bitter towards the British and deviously planted in the Nana Sahib's mind the seeds of rebellion.

A magic lantern image projector slide depicting a scene of Wheeler's entrenchment, which originally appeared in Mowbray Thomson's Cawnpore book.

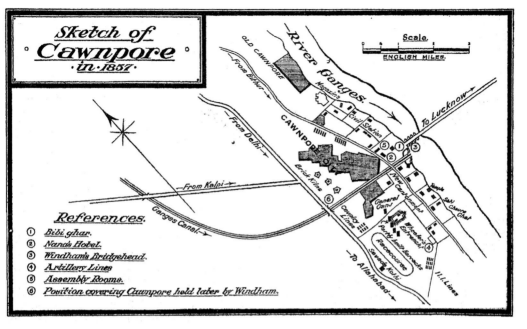

A basic sketch of Cawnpore showing the main areas associated with the siege and its aftermath.

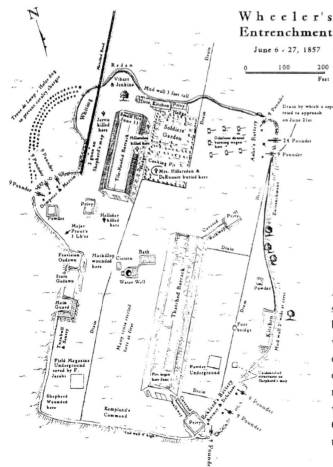

A map of the entrenchment showing the positions of the gun batteries and the two buildings, and where a number of other incidents occurred. The unfinished barracks occupied by Captain Thomson's men were situated to the left or west of the sketch, and the Sati Chaura Ghat was about a mile to the north-west.

On 23 June, the centenary of the battle of Plessey, the rebels made a dangerous assault on the entrenchment, led by the 2nd Native Cavalry and the 1st Native Infantry, which was repulsed by the defenders.

A photograph of the Barracks buildings after the siege, showing signs of severe damage from the constant heavy bombardments. The tile-roofed building is the one in the foreground. It seems that the two buildings were actually closer together than they are depicted in the sketch, and the north end of the soldiers' garden between the buildings can also be seen. The Trous de Loup would have been situated in the foreground.

The Sati Chaura Ghat – 'Hardeo's' or fishermans' temple. Jwala Pershad, one of the Nana's generals, was hanged beside the temple. There was a substantial memorial to the British victims there until independence in 1947, when it was dismantled and now lies at the bottom of the river.

A sketch depicting the chaotic scene as the British were fired upon as they tried to get away from the banks of the river at the Sati Chaura Ghat, and then most of them were cut to pieces by enemy cavalry.

A magic lantern image projector slide depicting Mowbray Thomson and others swimming for their lives in the River Ganges on 30 June 1857.

When news reached the Nana that a British boat had put up a good fight and had got away down the river, he sent three companies of infantry in pursuit of them in boats. They surrounded the British boat and brought them back to Cawnpore.

A sketch of the courtyard at the Bibighar. 'It was of one storey, with a court in the middle, and a tree grew in the court.'

A scene of the interior of the Bibighar where the atrocity took place. Lieutenant Crump produced a colour lithograph as he saw it on site at the time. It was entitled: The Chamber of Blood and became the template for all future sketches of the Bibighar interior, including this example.

The Bibighar well where the bodies of the dead were unceremoniously thrown after the massacre.

The Lindsay sisters. Caroline Ann (top right); Frances Davidson 'Fanny' (middle left); and Alice (bottom right). Their mother Kate was from Dundee, but they were living in Rochester before they sailed to India. Death from disease saved them all from the fate worse than death that the others had to suffer.

Isabel White, standing left, with two of the daughters of the Civil Service Judicial Commissioner at Oude. The picture appears in *The Lucknow Album*, held in the British Library. Isabel was the daughter of a Somerset brewery owner. She was in her late twenties, and had been persuaded to go to Cawnpore with the intention of finding a suitor among the eligible young men in the town. She became a victim of the Bibighar massacre.

Amy Horne and some of her siblings.

An engraved portrait of Lieutenant Frederick Saunders, a hero of the 84th Regiment, wearing the uniform of the Turkish Contingent in the Crimea. He almost succeeded in assassinating the Nana Sahib, but harsh retaliation caused him to suffer a brutal barbarous death.

Captain Edward Seppings of the 2nd Bengal Light Cavalry was the grandson of Sir Robert Seppings, a well-known naval architect. He and his family escaped in Vibart's boat, but they were re-captured and suffered a dreadful ordeal when they returned to Cawnpore.

An original water colour of Jessie Seppings. She was of Scottish descent, and went out to India as a young girl. She married Captain Seppings in 1849, and they had three boys, one of them being a new-born infant.

William Jonah Shepherd lost all his family during the events at Cawnpore, and was one of the very few people who lived to tell the tale.

Captain Mowbray Thomson was one of only five men known to have escaped the Cawnpore massacres. After reading several conflicting accounts concerning the incidents he decided to publish his own account in 1859. He rose to the rank of Lieutenant–General, and died in Reading in 1917.

A child's damaged black shoe recovered from the Bibighar. (*National Army Museum*)

This home-made toy belonged to John and Edward Seppings and accompanied them throughout their ordeal at Cawnpore. It is a small wooden snuff box containing two small wooden marbles. Apparently, a couple of Hindus who had been watching the dreadful events on the morning of 16 July, knowing whom the two little boys were, picked up the toy and gave it to Sir Henry Havelock and his men as they entered Cawnpore on 17 July. From there it found its way back to the Turnbull family and has remained with them ever since. (*Mark Probett*)

As Lt-Colonel William Gordon-Alexander of the 93rd Highlanders was on his way to the relief of Lucknow on 3 November 1857, he went to see the Bibighar house, during which he noticed a lock of hair attached to some prickly plants growing at the mouth of the well. He collected the hair and eventually had it mounted on a velvet board inside a glass case. (*National Army Museum*)

This wooden memorial is one of about 20 made by soldiers of the 32nd Regiment as they returned through Cawnpore from defending Lucknow, on 21 November 1857. They had left wives and children behind in Cawnpore and many were slaughtered there. The wood to make them is believed to have been taken from the main door of the Bibighar. (*Mark Probett*)

The small cross is believed to have been made by soldiers of the 32nd Regiment from the wood of the ranyan tree which hung over the well. (*Mark Probett*)

Tantia Tope shackled in captivity before he was executed on the public gallows at Shivpuri on 18 April 1859.

A lock of Tantia Tope's hair, which was taken at the time of his capture and execution. (*National Army Museum*)

The British dismantled the Bibighar house and grounds after the Rebellion was put down, and the area around it was cleared of trees.

A cast iron memorial railing and a cross were placed at the site of the Bibighar well.

The native inhabitants of Cawnpore were forced to pay a fine of thirty-thousand pounds for the creation of a permanent memorial, which was partial punishment for not going to the aid of the women and children in the Bibighar.

The marble centre-piece known as The Angel of the Resurrection was completed in 1865, and came to be the most visited historical site in British India; even more so than the Taj Mahal.

The Memorial Cross at Wheeler's sepulchral well, which was located about 80 paces to the south-west of the entrenchment, and under which the remains of about 350 people still rest. The well lies within a military zone about 35 paces from one of the old barrack buildings near Cambridge Road. It was overgrown and run down until it was taken over by a largely Christian regiment and restored to its original condition, including the newly-painted cast iron fence which surrounds it. (*Mark Probett*)

A brass plaque dedicated to Mowbray Thomson situated on a wall at All Souls Memorial Church in Cawnpore. (*Mark Probett*)

In honour of the British who lost their lives in the massacres, the All Soul's Memorial Church was completed in 1875. It contains fourteen memorial tablets with the known names of the victims. (*Mark Probett*)

The site is now within the Nana Rao Park, where the remains of a circular ridge of the well tomb can still be seen. A bust of Tantia Tope, which could have been sited somewhere else in the park, has been placed overlooking the well. (*Mark Probett*)

them all, along with Mr Jacobi and Mr Cox, who had formerly served with the 1st Bengal European Fusiliers.

Private White was walking with his wife, who had their two young twins, one in each arm, trying to stay under the shelter of a wall. However, a bullet hit White and passed right through him. It then passed right through his wife's arms and broke them. They all fell down in a heap and one of the babies was also injured. Captain Thomson stated:

> I saw her afterwards in the main guard lying on her back, with the two children laid one at each breast, while the mother's bosom refused not what her arms had no power to administer. Assuredly no imagination or invention ever devised such pictures as this most horrible siege was constantly presenting to our view.

Unfortunately, the forebodings of Major Evans at Lucknow came to reality as his wife was killed when an enemy round shot smashed into a masonry wall and a mass of bricks that became displaced came crashing down onto her. Their two children also died in the entrenchment.

It was noted that Lieutenant Jervis of the engineers always insisted in taking his time as he went about his duties. However, his luck ran out as he was walking between the tile-roofed barracks and Whiting's battery when he came under a hail of bullets and was hit and killed.

The Reverend Moncrieff:

> '… was most indefatigable in the performance of his ministry of mercy with the wounded and the dying. Public worship of any combined form was quite out of the question, but this devoted clergyman went from post to post reading prayers while we stood to arms.'
>
> The Romish priest was the only well-fed man in our party, for the Irish privates used to contribute from their scanty rations for his support.'

Captain Thomson stated that the Reverend 'died from sunstroke or apoplexy about halfway through the siege, but there is a report that he was killed at the ghat with his wife and child.

Amy Horne asserted that 'The Reverend William Haycock died raving mad through the combined effects of heat, exposure and fear, and used to walk about stark naked. His condition was pitiful to see.'

Under cover of darkness, a sergeant and four men were employed to dig shallow graves at various convenient places around the entrenchment so they would only need to convey the dead bodies from where they fell for about twenty paces or so to bury them.

At various times during the siege a number of natives had been captured and this total had now reached eleven. They were shackled together by their wrists near the main guard. As provisions became low it was suggested to shoot them, but instead they had been spared and for about an hour they were placed under the watchful eye of Bridget Widdowson, the formidable wife of Private Thomas Widdowson of the 32nd Light Infantry, who was described as 'a stout, muscular, sergeant-major of a woman'. She stood over them with a drawn sword, in such a menacing way that they were too scared to move. They were so fearful of her that as soon as she was relieved of her duty they all tried to escape!

According to Lieutenant Thomson, the Barrack 4 was the most perilous to be defending at first. Sixteen men, including the two vicar's sons, Alfred Heberden and William La Touch, were among several railway engineers who defended this building for three days without any military supervision, during which time they, 'Distinguished themselves greatly by their skills and courage', particularly their marksmanship.

On numerous occasions rebels in large numbers used the cover of the walls to try creep up on the railwaymen and overwhelm them, but each time they tried they received serious casualties, and they only managed to occupy Barrack 1 because it was the nearest to their forces to the north, and all the Barracks from number 5 to number 9 were occupied by rebels moving forward from the south.

After a few days, Lieutenant Jenkins was sent to command them, and Lieutenant Glanville was sent with sixteen men to occupy Barrack 2, which was strategically the most important because it was only 200 paces from the entrenchment. This building then became the most dangerous position, and soon Lieutenant Glanville was dangerously wounded. He was taken into Barrack 4 to be attended by Surgeon Daniel MacAuley, and Captain Elms took over command. He in turn was requested by

Captain Moore to take up another duty. Before he left he gave his watch to Lieutenant Thomson so he could tell the time of day, and left the lieutenant in command of Barrack 2. He stated 'It was most harassing work to stand hour after hour, watching for the approach of the rebels … As soon as night set in all hands were required on the lookout and we stood through the weary hours with muskets at the charge, peering out into the darkness.' With him was Ensign Henderson, with about half a dozen men each of the 84th Regiment and the Madras Fusiliers, and two railway plate-layers.

Because they were so close to the enemy positions, most of these men were killed, but as it was such an important position, as soon as Captain Moore received notification of the loss he sent over any man he could spare, military or civilian, as a replacement.

As the siege wore on, Lieutenant Thomson and some men erected a 'crow's nest' from items of wood they found around the place, and built it to about 20ft. Lieutenant Stirling, who came from a gallant family associated with the Victoria Cross, thought nothing of exposing himself to enemy sniper fire, and he willingly manned this elevated position for many hours at a time, shooting with great accuracy at anything he saw moving against the buildings from the rebel strongholds. Lieutenant Thomson stated that he lost count of the number of the enemy he killed.

All the ammunition for the outposts was supplied by volunteers, who ran the gauntlet of fire from the enemy in Barrack 1, as they ran towards the entrenchment. Lieutenant Thomson described the situation as thus 'It was no trifle under any circumstances, to hop, skip, and jump, to the covering place at half the distance in the open, but the ammunition bearers were exposed to conditions that any insurance company would write down doubly-hazardous.' And yet, as he concluded 'There was no difficulty however, in obtaining the services of men willing to undertake the perilous but necessary duty.'

On 14 June, the garrison suffered a serious setback when the roof of the thatched barrack was set on fire, destroying the few medical supplies, as well as the jackets of the soldiers of the 32nd, who could afterwards be seen poking through the ashes looking for lost medals. Moore immediately determined to 'give the enemy an early and a convincing proof that the spirit of our people was not broken by this great calamity':

At the dead of night ensuing he stole out from the entrenchment with fifty picked men at his heels in the direction of the chapel and the racket-court. Beginning from this point, the party hurried down the rebel lines under favour of the darkness, doing whatever rapid mischief was possible. They surprised in untimely slumber some native gunners, who never waked again; spiked and rolled over several twenty-four pounders; gratified their feelings by blowing up a piece which had given them special annoyance; and got back, carrying in their arms four of their number and leaving one behind.

It was still possible to get messages out of the entrenchment to Lucknow, which was done by rolling them up very small and concealing them in an orifice of Hindu messengers; usually in an ear or up a nostril. These messengers faced great peril along the 40 miles of roads between the two cities, and anyone who was intercepted and caught by the rebels while doing this was likely to no longer have any ears or nose.

On the night of 14 June General Wheeler sent the following to Martin Gubbins:

We have been besieged since the 6th by the Nana Sahib, joined by the whole of the native troops, who broke out on the morning of the fourth. The enemy have two 24-pounders, and several other guns. We have only eight 9-pounders. The whole of the Christian population is with us in a temporary entrenchment, and our defence has been noble and wonderful; our loss heavy and cruel. We want aid, aid, aid! Regards to Lawrence.

PS: If we had 200 men we could punish the scoundrels and aid you.

The reply was extremely negative, and a disappointed General Wheeler asked his second in command to answer it, so on the night of 18 June Captain Moore sent back the following:

By desire of Sir Hugh Wheeler, I have the honour to acknowledge your letter of the 16th.

Sir Hugh regrets you cannot send him the 200 men as he believes with their assistance we could drive the insurgents from Cawnpore, and capture their guns.

Our troops, officers and volunteers have acted most nobly, and on several occasions a handful of men have driven hundreds before them. Our loss has been chiefly from the sun, and heavy guns. Our rations will last a fortnight, and we are still well supplied with ammunition. Our guns are serviceable. Report says that troops are advancing from Allahabad, and any assistance might save our garrison. We, of course, are prepared to hold out till the last. It is needless to mention the name of those who have been killed, or died.

We trust in God, and if our exertions here assist your safety, it will be a consolation to know that our friends appreciate our devotion. Any news of relief will cheer us.

On the last Sunday of the siege, 21 June, Major Vibart sent a letter to Lucknow, stating:

We have been cannonaded for six hours a day by twelve guns. This evening, in three hours, upwards of thirty shells (mortars) were thrown into the entrenchment. This has occurred daily for the last eight days, an idea may be formed of our casualties, and how little protection the barracks afford to the women. Any aid, to be effective must be immediate. In event of rain falling, our position would be untenable.

According to telegraphic despatches received previous to the outbreak, thousand Europeans were to have been here on the fourteenth instant. This force may be on its way. Any assistance you can send might co-operate with it. Nine-pounder ammunition, chiefly cartridges, is required. Should the above force arrive, we can, in return, insure the safety of Lucknow. Being simply a military man, Colonel Wheeler has no power to offer bribes in land and money to the insurgents, nor any means whatever of communicating with them.

You can ascertain the best means of crossing the river. Nujuffgurh Ghat is suggested. It is earnestly requested that whatever is done may be effected without a moments delay. We have lost about a third of our original number. The enemy are strongest in artillery. They appear not have more than about four hundred or five hundred infantry. They move their guns with difficulty, by means of unbroken bullocks. The infantry are great cowards and are easily repulsed.

At about midday on 21 June, Lieutenant de la Fosse showed great bravery in extinguishing the flames of a burning ammunition wagon, which was under heavy fire from the enemy. He was stationed at Lieutenant Eckford's south-east battery when an enemy shot landed in the back of a gun carriage and blew it up, and bits of burning wood began to cascade over the area. Having got the range, the enemy's eighteen and twenty-four-pounder gun crews, apparently six in number, started to bombard the area, putting the battery's stacks of ammunition shells in great peril. With complete disregard for his own safety, Lieutenant de la Fosse immediately ran over to the danger area, clambered under the wagon and, gathering earth with both hands, he managed to dampen out the flames. Two other men carrying buckets of water followed him in the dangerous task and the gallant lieutenant doused out the last few flaming embers.

On another occasion, Lieutenant de la Fosse noticed that a small enemy gun situated at Barracks 1 was causing problems. He had been forced to load his nine-pounder with six-pounder shells, and consequently it was difficult to get any accuracy on his firing. Having been frustrated for days at this, he decided to load the gun with three six-pounder shells and a stocking full of grape shot, and rammed it down tight. Hoping that such a load would not burst the weapon, he fired it at the enemy gun and blasted it out of action.

The rebels made sorties against the entrenchment every day, and although they were always repulsed, the losses were sometimes heavy and considerably reduced the number of men able to keep up the defence.

The night of 22 June was the eve of the centenary of the battle of Plassey, when Robert Clive defeated Indian forces in one of the main battles that led to the expansion of British rule in the sub-continent. One of the driving forces of the rebellion was a prophecy that predicted the downfall of the East India Company's rule 100 years after Plassey. This prompted the rebels to prepare for a major attack.

British sentries noticed more activity among the rebels occupying Barracks 5 to 9, adjacent to the entrenchment, and their numbers were increasing. One sentry reported seeing as many as 700 rebels sneaking up to the barrack buildings, and it has been suggested that as many as 1,000 were ready to make an assault. They launched attacks to try to occupy the Barracks the British were defending, and at one critical point Lieutenant Thomson sent to Captain Moore's headquarters with a request for reinforcements 'But Moore replied that he could spare nobody except himself and Lieutenant de la Fosse.' When they arrived they at once got together some volunteers and launched an assault, Moore was armed with a sword and de la Fosse with an empty musket. As they advanced the captain shouted out 'Number One to the front!' a well-known word of command that caused the rebels to think that the British were counter-attacking with rifles and fixed bayonets. The ploy worked and the defenders 'Expelled the rebels from the barracks they had seized,' and they 'ran like rabbits'.

During the operation, Lieutenants Thompson and Daniell heard some scuffling in one of the rooms, and as they rushed in together they saw Captain Moore on the ground in the grasp of a powerful native. The rebel was about to cut the throat of the second in command when Daniell surged forward and bayoneted him.

As Lieutenant Thomson and Captain Jenkins moved around the barracks to check that all the buildings had been cleared, the captain received a terrible injury. Lieutenant Thomson remembered:

> … Captain Jenkins and I were … surveying the effects of the sortie we had just concluded … between the barracks numbered 4 and 5, a wounded sepoy, who had feigned death … suddenly raised his musket and shot Captain Jenkins through the jaw. I had the miserable satisfaction of first dismissing the assailant, and then conducted my suffering companion to his barrack. He lived two or three days in excruciating agony, and then died from exhaustion. In Captain Jenkins we lost one of the bravest, and one of the best of our party.

It was at this time that Lieutenant Thomson was injured 'I had a memento of 23 of June in the shape of a wound in the left thigh from a grape-shot, which ploughed up the flesh, but happily, though narrowly, escaped the bone.'

At first light the 2nd Cavalry launched a determined charge against the northern sections of the entrenchment, making sure they avoided the *trous de loup*, but when they got to within fifty paces they were repulsed with canister shot. Then sepoys of the 1st Infantry under the command of Subadar-Major Radhay Singh advanced under cover of cotton bales and parapets, but their leader was shot down with the first volley from the entrenchment, and the bales caught fire from the canisters and became more of a hazard to them. Some of their infantry made an attack against the entrenchment opposite the barracks and managed to get close enough to engage in hand-to-hand combat with Lieutenant Thomson and sixteen other men, but they couldn't get beyond British cold steel. The rebels failed to gain an entry and they retreated, leaving twenty-five of their men lying dead around the defences.

On this, and many other occasions, Lieutenant Ashe directed the guns in his battery with superb accuracy. Lieutenant Thomson stated that Ashe was 'A great scourge to our enemies, in consequence of the surprising celerity and accuracy of the firing from his gun.' After every round he would 'jump up onto the heel of the gun, regardless of the exposure, that he might see the extent of the damage he had inflicted'. There is little doubt that his bravery would have inspired great confidence in his men.

Caroline Edith Moore was one of the several celebrated heroines of the siege. Historians recorded how 'Her splendid courage and fortitude endeared her to every man, woman and child within the entrenchment,' and:

> When the vicissitudes of battle called her husband to the outposts, Mrs Moore would step across with her work, and spend the day beneath a little hut of bamboos covered with canvas, which the garrison of Barrack 2 had raised for her in their most sheltered corner. Seldom had fair lady a less appropriate bower.
>
> Generally morale was low, and in their despair some members of the garrison attempted suicide. Lieutenant Thomson wrote: 'Faces that had been beautiful became chiselled with deep furrows. Some were slowly sinking into the settled vacancy of look which marked insanity.' All now were in 'tattered clothing, begrimed with dirt, emaciated in countenance'. Yet in Captain Moore 'hope shone like a pillar of fire when it had gone out in all others'.

He continued to give encouragement to these sorry people, in addition to carrying out his dangerous duties in the outposts and attending to his responsibilities as a husband and father of two young children forced to endure 'the horrors of a nightmare'.

Lieutenant Thomson stated:

Seventeen days and nights our little party had resisted all the efforts made by the overwhelming numbers of the foe to storm the position. There remained nothing now for them to do but to starve us out; henceforth they abandoned all attempts to take us by assault.

Prisoners taken from the sepoys always gave utterance to profuse exclamations of wonder at our holding out from day to day as we did, and looked upon the cause as something altogether supernatural; they had all felt sure that we must be overpowered by their numbers, or at least be utterly destroyed by the intense heat of the season. This last opinion will not be thought unreasonable when I say that it was often quite impossible to touch the barrel of a gun, and once or twice muskets went off at midday, either from the sun exploding their caps or from the fiery heat of the metal.

The British had kept their discipline and shown the usual resilience they always did when they had their backs to the wall. Like the men at Rorke's Drift during the Zulu War of 1879, a mixture of experienced officers who kept their cool in difficult circumstances and the dogged determination of the younger men not to give in had succeeded in demoralising the enemy.

As a Eurasian, Jonah Shepherd volunteered to act as a spy or to open negotiations, and sneaked out of the entrenchment disguised as a cook. He was captured soon after, although the rebels did not realise he had come from within the entrenchment. He was tried by the mutineers and imprisoned for a sentence of three years with hard labour, being shackled in irons.

During the horrors of the siege Ann Fraser won the admiration of all our party by her continuous and caring attention to the wounded. 'Neither danger nor fatigue seemed to have power to suspend her ministry of mercy.'

John Mackillop had previously stated that he was not a fighting man, but he made himself useful where he could, and, accordingly, he took up the task of drawing water from the well, mainly on behalf of the parched women and children. For a whole week he managed to do this, even though he came under enemy sniper fire every time he attempted it. Several times he would run the gauntlet of enemy fire with bullets falling short and sending up little spurts of earth, and while others went over his head with a shrill whistle. Inevitably, as the women heard the clanging of the ladle in the water bucket approaching and expected to have their thirst quenched very soon, the sound of metal on metal suddenly stopped. John had been hit in the groin and dangerously wounded by a grape shot. His last words were an earnest entreaty that someone would go and draw water for a lady to whom he had promised it.

Being the son of a vicar, Alfred Heberden decided to take over the compassionate task of distributing the water. However, he suffered a similar fate when a bullet passed through both of his hips. He was rushed into the surgery barracks, where he 'lay for a whole week upon his face in agony'. However, according to witnesses he suffered in silence as much as he could.

Some members of the artillery were much more mercenary as they paid the Christian drummers 'a trifle' to fetch water that they would then sell to the families. However, a 'very nice, well-made' drummer named Charlie O'Dwyer could not bear the cries for water from the children any longer, so he decided to risk the bullets and make a few runs to the well on their behalf. After one of the runs, he decided to lay down for a while to get his breath back, and as he did so a shell landed directly into the cistern and on exploding it maimed him in several places.

A spy entered the entrenchment in the guise of a water carrier, and carried a report back to rebel leaders that the British were desperately short of food and much reduced in numbers, and they might be willing to surrender. A short letter was drawn up and on 25th it was delivered to General Wheeler by the wife of a Eurasian merchant held prisoner by Nana Sahib, said to have been Mrs Greenaway, carrying a child in her arms, and escorted by a troop of the 4th Light Cavalry carrying a white flag. The letter was addressed to 'The subjects of Her Most Gracious Majesty, Queen Victoria', and read 'All those who are in no way connected with the acts of Lord Dalhousie, and are willing to lay down their arms, shall receive safe passage to Allahabad.' Only Henry Jacobi would have been adversely affected by this, and he had died of smallpox on 10 June.

General Wheeler was irritated by its tone, and together with a number of younger officers was in favour of rejecting it outright. Lieutenant Saunders 'raised his voice against putting any trust in the word of the rebels, and was for continuing the struggle to the last'. However, Captain Moore, who had taken over the direction of the defence after Wheeler and other senior officers had become incapacitated, prudently pointed out that the wet weather was due, which would soon wash away the mud walls of the entrenchment, fill up the rifle pits and dampen the remaining powder, making the continuation of the defence impossible.

On the next day Captain Moore and some other officers met the Nana's men, also carrying a white flag. The meeting took place without any trouble, and on their return to the entrenchment they told the general the Nana's terms and what he intended to do.

They were to surrender their guns and ammunition, retaining only their hand arms and sixty rounds, and all their remaining treasure. They were to leave the entrenchment peacefully and be escorted down to the Sati Chaura Ghat on the banks of the Ganges, from where they would be allowed to travel to Allahabad unmolested.

Ghats are a kind of riverside pier that have long been a traditional part of Indian religious life. They usually consist of a landing stage with a series of steps leading down from a temple to a jetty on the banks of a holy river, such as the Ganges. The Sati Chaura Ghat was on the southern side of the River Ganges, marking the most northern boundary of the city.

The general was eventually persuaded to accept that it was their only real chance of survival, so late morning of the next day a tent was put up and during a four-hour meeting Captain Moore and five other officers presented a treaty, which was the British response to the Nana's proposition.

During the talks a sepoy suggested to Captain Whiting that not one man, woman or child would go safe to Allahabad. On his return to the camp the captain told Captain Moore, who is said to have dismissed it as rubbish, and that all would be safe.

That evening there was an eerie silence at Cawnpore, the like of which the British had not enjoyed for three weeks. Lieutenant Master scribbled a note to his father, the commanding officer of the 7th Light Cavalry, at Lucknow:

> 'We have now held out for twenty-one days under a tremendous fire. The Rajah of Bithoor has offered to forward us in safety to Allahabad, and the General has accepted his terms. I am all right, though twice wounded. Charlotte Newnham and Bella Blair are dead. I'll write from Allahabad. God bless you.'

Chapter 8

The Traitor's Gate

A deputation of officers went down to the Sati Chaura Ghat to see what arrangements the rebel leaders had made for the evacuation of the garrison by boat to Allahabad.

The head bearer of Colonel Williams, who was in command of the 56th Native Infantry before the mutiny, stated:

Even after the cessation of hostilities, we were not allowed to go and see our masters. On the morning of the twenty-sixth of June, three officers of the Fifty-Sixth, (Lieutenants) (Charles) Goad, (Hornby) Fagan and (Henry) Warde, mounted on elephants, and two Europeans, whose names and regiments I don't know, mounted on another elephant, came out of the entrenchment and went to the river to inspect the boats.

The gardener and I, taking some grapes, went up to the officers, and told them that we were in a starving condition and wanted to come to our masters in the entrenchment. They said, 'No, you can't come with us, but we shall come out tomorrow and you shall accompany us to Allahabad in boats.' Goad Sahib and Warde Sahib gave me each two rupees. They told me that my master had died a natural death; that my mistress was well, but slightly wounded; and that Miss Mary was dead. Her death was caused by fright at the cannonade, and that she was not wounded.

The other two men mentioned by the head bearer were Captain Turner and Lieutenant de la Fosse. When they arrived at the river they saw that about forty boats had been made ready for the evacuation.

After some negotiation it was agreed that the garrison would give up the entrenchment and march down to the ghat under arms on the 27th. They were provided with all kinds of transport to take them to the river, but they were ordered to give up all their valuables and treasure, and it was agreed that they were to take their rifles and sixty rounds of ammunition each. Early on the morning of Saturday, 27 June they got themselves in readiness to make their way down to the River Ganges.

Captain Moore passed between the ragged groups of survivors, impressing upon them the necessity of getting directly into the boats as soon as they reached the ghat, and pushing off immediately. He evidently suspected a trap. Watched by swarms of natives who had come from the city to see the procession go by, Moore placed himself at the head of an advanced guard of the 32nd, and led out the bedraggled garrison. They left more than 200 of their friends and relatives buried in the entrenchment, together with the bodies of eleven more lying on quilts 'Some still breathing, though dying from severe gunshot wounds.'

Colonel Williams's head bearer continued:

On the twenty-seventh of June, a little before 6am, as many as could walk came out; some of the wounded in dhoolies, others of whom were left behind. The party from the entrenchment was surrounded by sepoys. I had great difficulty in reaching my mistress. I applied to Annundeedee, the havildar of the Fifty-sixth, who said the thing was impossible. I appealed to him, and begged him to remember the kindness he had received from the colonel. After persuasion, he said that he could not show his face before the colonel's lady, but directed four sepoys to take me to my mistress, and prevent my being disturbed.

I was then taken to my mistress, with whom were her two daughters, Miss Georgiana, and Miss Fanny. They were in a wretched plight; scorched and blistered by the sun. My mistress had a slight bullet wound on the upper lip. She said that my master had died on the eighth of June. My mistress then asked about the property left in the house, and inquired about all the servants, and especially after the cook. She then told me to go and fetch him, as she wanted him to go down to Allahabad with her; and told me to go to her son in the Hills, and inform him of all that had occurred. She told me to make every endeavour to join her son as soon as the roads should be open, and to show him the spot where the colonel was buried. I told her I did not know the spot. She said the groom who had remained with them in the entrenchment would show it to me.

Although it is impossible for Jonah Shepherd to have witnessed the plight of Colonel Ewart and Emma, he said that the wounded officer was being carried in a palanquin with Emma walking by the side. The bearers struggled to keep up with the rest and eventually fell back quite a distance. As they were passing the church some onlookers became hostile and some rebels mocked him in a sham parade. An eyewitness stated that Colonel Ewart and Emma were murdered soon afterwards.

All evidence suggests that it was Tantia Tope who took control of the situation at the ghat, along with Jwala Prasad and Teeka Singh. On the orders of Tantia Tope, a bell sounded and acts of dreadful treachery began.

Amy Horne described what happened next:

We found that the boats were not very close to the shore, and there were no gangways, and the task of getting on board was a most difficult one. We had to wade knee-deep through the water, and it was pitiful to witness the difficulty of the aged, the sick, and the wounded in clambering up the boats' sides.

While we were endeavouring to embark the shore was lined with spectators, and after all had embarked the word was given to proceed. Instead of the crews obeying the order, a signal was given from the shore, and they all leapt into the water and waded to the bank, after having first secreted burning charcoal in the thatch of most of the boats. Immediately a volley of bullets assailed us, followed by a hail of shot and grape. In a few minutes pandemonium reigned. The boats were seen to be wrapped in flames, and the wounded were burnt to death. Some jumped overboard and tried to swim to the opposite shore, but were picked off by the bullets of the sepoys. Others were drowned, while a few others jumped into the water and hid behind their boats to escape the pitiless fire. But the guns continued their vile work, and grape and musketry were poured into the last mentioned people from the opposite bank which soon became alive with rebels, placed there to intercept the refugees to that shore. A few succeeded in pushing their boats to the further side of the river and were mercilessly slaughtered.

The cavalry waded into the river with drawn swords and cut down those who were still alive, while the infantry boarded the boats to loot.

Amy also described how a Mr Kirkpatrick was:

very horribly mutilated while wading to the boat. The rebels made several cuts at his neck, chopped off his hands, which he held up to protect his head, the swords being blunt and the blows awkwardly dealt, this poor man's tortures are beyond description. I saw him about half-an-hour later lying in the water still alive!

She notes that:

Our poor old General, Sir Hugh Wheeler, suffered the same fate: his hands were cut off as soon as he was brought from the boat. The act becomes a symbolic emasculation: with their hands cut off, the power of British men is nullified.

The air resounded with the shrieks of the women and children, and agonising prayers to God for mercy. The water was red with blood, and the smoke from the heavy firing of the cannon and muskets and the fire from the burning boats lay like dense clouds all around us. Several men were mutilated in the presence of their wives, while babes and children were torn from their mother's arms and hacked to pieces.

Private Murphy stated that he saw General Wheeler and his family making their way into the water to get into one of the boats when the firing started. He was seized and dragged away, and Murphy did not see what happened to him after that.

However, according to Trevelyan, his fate was also recorded by Mrs Bradshaw, and apparently confirmed by Mrs Setts:

In the boat where I was to have gone were the schoolmistress and twenty-two missies, General Wheeler came last in a palkee [a kind of

covered stretcher carried by several bearers]. They carried him into
the water near the boat. I stood close by. He said: 'Carry me a little
further towards the boat.' But a trooper said: 'No, get out here!' As
the general got out of the palkee, head foremost, the trooper gave
him a cut with his sword into the neck, and he fell into the water.

Lieutenant de la Fosse reported 'Two guns that had been hidden were run
out and opened on us immediately, whilst sepoys came from all directions
and kept up a brisk fire.'

All except three of the forty or so boats got clear of the shallows, the
majority having been purposely grounded. The first boat drifted fatally
towards the far bank, which was lined with rebels, and as they came under
fire the second boat was hit below the waterline by a round shot.

A third boat, commanded by Major Vibart, fared better. Captain Moore
was killed by a musket ball through the heart while trying to push the
boat away from the bank, and as Lieutenants Ashe and Boulton waded in
to take his place and they too were shot down. However, Vibart's boat was
able to float away from the bank and across the water to come alongside
the second boat and take off some of the survivors.

The boatmen had made sure that they discarded the oars into the river,
and the only implements that could be found to propel the vessel were, as
Mowbray Thomson recorded, 'a spar or two and such pieces of wood as
we could in safety tear from the sides. Grape and round shot flew about
us from either river bank; and shells burst constantly on the sandbanks.'

Lieutenant Thomson remembered:

Ann Fraser escaped to the boats with scarcely any clothing on her.
In the thickest of the deadly volleys she again appeared indifferent
to danger and to her own scanty covering; while with perfect
equanimity and unperturbed fortitude she was entirely occupied in
the attempt to soothe and relieve the agonised sufferers around her,
whose wounds scarcely made their condition worse than her own.
Such rare heroism deserves a far higher tribute than this simple
record from my pen.

Lieutenant Thomson stated that Lieutenant Harrison:

> … left one of the boats in company with a number of passengers, and by wading they reached a small island, about two hundred yards from the shore. While I was swimming past this islet I saw three sowars of cavalry who had also waded from the Cawnpore bank. One of them cut down one of our women with his tulwar, and then made off for Harrison, who received him with a charge from his revolver, and waited for the second man, whom he despatched in like manner, whereupon the third took to the water on the shore-side of the ait, and Harrison, plunging in on the river side, swam to Vibart's boat.

Lieutenant Thomson concluded 'Lieutenant Harrison was shot dead. I took off his rings and gave them to Mrs Seppings, as I thought the women might perhaps excite some commiseration, and that if any of our party escaped, it would be some of them.'

Private Murphy threw off all his clothes but for his trousers and began to swim to Vibart's boat as it was drifting in the middle of the river about 100 yards away. However, he saw that several enemy cavalrymen were pushing through the water on their horses in his direction. When they got to within about 10 yards of him, he quickly dived down to the river bed and began to crawl along the bottom for as long as he could hold his breath. When he became desperate for air he swam to the surface and realised that he had got about 200 yards away from them. Unfortunately they saw him and gave whip and spur to their mounts to chase after him again. He realised that his trousers were restricting him from making progress in the water, so he took them off and got away faster. Eventually the horses got tired from pushing through the water and his assailants gave up and went back to join in the slaughter at the ghat.

Thomson, de la Fosse, Gunner Sullivan of the Bengal Artillery, and Private Murphy of the 84th Regiment, were the only male survivors from Vibart's boat. They were sent ashore by Vibart after the boat grounded at Najafgarh to fight off their pursuers, which they succeeded in doing, but on returning to the boat they found it had gone.

When news had reached the Nana that a British boat had put up a good fight and had got away down the river, he sent three companies of the 1st Oudh Infantry in pursuit of them in boats. They surrounded the British boat and brought them back to Cawnpore. According to a spy named Myoor Tewarree of the 1st Bengal Native Infantry, there were fifty men, twenty-five women and four children (one boy and three half-grown girls). He also stated that General Wheeler was with this party.

Sadly for Jonah Shepherd, he overheard from his rebel-held prison cell that his entire family had been murdered – probably at Sati Chaura Ghat 'Consisting of wife and daughter (my infant daughter having died from a musket shot in the head) two nieces, a sister and her infant son, a brother, and two old ladies.'

Lieutenant Saunders had succeeded in clambering into a boat, but quickly jumped overboard in midstream in order to get away from the inferno of heat caused by the fire on the blazing roof. On reaching the shore, he was seized by the rebels and stripped of his sword. However, he managed to conceal his fully loaded revolver in his uniform. It is not known how he bargained for his life, perhaps owing to his commanding manner, but he escaped the fate of the majority of other adult male survivors who were at once rounded up and shot. The women and children (including Sarah Saunders and young Frederick), who survived the initial slaughter were among the people who were taken off to the Nana's headquarters at the Savada House.

Saunders demanded an audience with Nana Sahib, and a few soldiers of the 84th, who had 'determined to share the fate of their commander', were brought before the rebel leader. There, in a gallant show of defiance, he dashed forward through the guards by whom he was surrounded, shooting down five of them with his revolver, and attempted to assassinate the Nana by firing the sixth round at him, but unfortunately without effect, as reports stated that he either missed or the gun failed to fire. He was quickly seized and thrown to the floor, where he was stretched out and crucified by having his hands and knees nailed to the ground, and his nose, ears, hands and feet were viciously cut off. He was then left mutilated, bleeding and roasting in the sun and all through the night until the next day, when further and more horrible cruelties were perpetrated. A body of cavalry charged over him, each man of which cut at him as he passed, until his body was literally hewn into pieces. It is not known at what point death relieved him from his unutterable agony.

According to a newspaper report, 'Lieutenant Saunders left a wife and two sons to weep his loss, and a wide circle of friends to hold in honoured remembrance his terribly glorious end.'

Most of the men brought back to Cawnpore had been seriously wounded. Major Edward Vibart nursed a wounded arm, Captain Athill Turner had both his legs smashed, Lieutenant Richard Owen Quinn was shot through the arm, and Lieutenant Masters was shot in the thigh. Doctor Boyes and his wife were also there. Captain Seppings had been wounded in both arms, and his wife, Jessie, was nursing a gunshot wound to the thigh. One of their two sons continued to clutch a makeshift toy throughout the ordeal, consisting of two wooden balls contained in a wooden snuff box. Susan Blair and young Susan were also present.

A note in the Blairs' Bible found in the Bibighar, which had seemingly gone on the journey to Soorajpore and back to Cawnpore, stated they were brought back and taken out of the boat on the night of 29 June, and then they were taken to the Savada Kothi on the morning of 30 June and presented before the Nana Sahib.

The men were separated from the women and were told to sit on the ground, and the order was given that all the males should be executed by sepoys of the 1st Bengal Native Infantry, who placed themselves standing over the British men and prepared to fire.

Then Kate Boyes called out 'I will not leave my husband, and if he must die I will die along with him.' She ran to her husband and sat down behind him, clasping him tightly around his waist. This prompted some of the other women to run over and do the same. The men told them 'Go! Go!' and the Nana ordered his soldiers to get them away and they were grabbed by the arms and forcibly removed, but Kate gripped Doctor Boyes so tightly that they could not pull her away and she remained where she was, 'One of the most touching incidents of the Cawnpore story.'

As a firing squad began to prepare again, one of the captives asked for a short amount of time to pray and read some verses of comfort to his fellow humans. Some sources say this was a chaplain, while others say it was Captain Seppings acting as a padre. The Nana granted the request, and his hands were released just enough to take a small Bible or psalm book from his pocket. As he began to read another man, who had been wounded in the arm and leg, called out 'If you mean to kill us why don't you get on with it? Be quick, and get the work done at once. Why wait?'

When the passages from the Bible were finished the sepoys opened fire. As they were hit by bullets some rolled one way and some another, and those who did not die from the bullets were finished off with sabre strokes. The bodies were stripped of their clothing and valuables, and after lying exposed to the heat for several days they were dragged away and thrown into the Ganges.

After returning to find that Major Vibart's boat had gone, Lieutenant Thomson took up the story of what happened to him and his three companions afterwards:

> Our only hope of safety now was in flight; and, with a burning sun overhead, a rugged raving ground, and no covering for the feet, it was no easy task for our half-famished party to make head; but a rabble of riots and sepoys at our heels soon put all deliberation upon the course to be pursued, as it did ourselves, to flight. For about three miles we retreated, when I saw a temple in the distance, and gave orders to make for that. To render us less conspicuous as marks for the guns, we had separated to the distance of about twenty paces apart; from time to time loading and firing as we best could upon the multitude in our rear.
>
> As he was entering the temple, Sergeant Grady was shot through the head. I instantly set four of the men crouching down in the doorway with bayonets fixed, and their muskets so placed as to form a chevalde [rise in the narrow entrance]. The mob came on helter-skelter in such maddening haste that some of them fell or were pushed on to the bayonets, and their transfixed bodies made the barrier impassable to the rest, upon whom we, from behind our novel defence, poured shot upon shot into the crowd. The situation was the more favourable to us, in consequence of the temple having been built upon a base of brickwork three feet from the ground, and approached by steps on one side. The brother of Baboo Barn Buksh, who was leading the mob, was slain here; and his bereaved relation was pleased to send word to the Nana that the English were thoroughly invincible.

Foiled in their attempts to enter our asylum, they next began to dig at its foundation; but the walls had been well laid, and were not so easily to be moved as they expected. They now fetched faggots, and from the circular construction of the building they were able to place them right in front of the doorway with impunity, there being no window or loop-hole in the place through which we could attack them, nor any means of so doing, without exposing ourselves to the whole mob at the entrance. In the centre of the temple there was an altar for the presentation of gifts to the presiding deity; his shrine, however, had not lately been enriched, or it had more recently been visited by his ministering priests, for there were no gifts upon it. There was, however, in a deep hole in the centre of the stone which constituted the altar, a hollow with a pint or two of water in it, which, although long since putrid, we bailed out with our hands, and sucked down with great avidity. When the pile of faggots had reached the top of the doorway, or nearly so, they set them on fire, expecting to suffocate us; but a strong breeze kindly sent the great body of the smoke away from the interior of the temple. Fearing that the suffocating sultry atmosphere would be soon insupportable, I proposed to the men to sell their lives as dearly as possible; but we stood until the wood had sunk down into a pile of embers, and we began to hope that we might brave out their torture till night (apparently the only friend left us) would let us get out for food and attempted escape.

But their next expedient compelled an evacuation, for they brought bags of gunpowder, and threw them upon the red hot ashes. Delay would have been certain suffocation – so out we rushed. The burning wood terribly marred our bare feet, but it was no time to think of trifles. Jumping the parapet, we were in the thick of the rabble in an instant; we fired a volley, and ran a-muck with the bayonet. Seven of our number succeeded in reaching the bank of the river, and we first threw in our guns and then ourselves. The weight of ammunition we had in the pouches carried us under the water; while we were thus submerged we escaped the first volley that they fired. We slipped off the belts, rose again, and swam; and by the time they had loaded a second time, there were only heads for them to aim at. I turned round, and saw the banks of the river thronged with the black multitude, yelling, howling, and firing at us; while others of their party rifled the bodies of the six poor fellows we had left behind. Presently two more were shot in the head; and one private, Ryan, almost sinking from exhaustion, swam into a sandbank and was knocked on the head by two or three ruffians waiting to receive him. These villains had first promised Lieutenant De La Fosse and private Murphy that if they would come to the shore they should be protected, and have food given to them. They were so much inclined to yield that they made towards the bank, but suddenly and wisely altered their determination. Infuriated with disappointment, one of them threw his club at De La Fosse; but in the height of his energy lost his balance and fell into deep water; the other aimed at Murphy, and struck him on the heel. For two or three hours, we continued swimming; often changing our position, and the current our progress. At length our pursuers gave up the chase; a sowar on horseback was the last we saw of them.

When Captain Thomson led this valorous attack and retreat he was suffering from a gunshot wound in the head received on board the boat, having been twice before wounded in the defence of Cawnpore. After swimming 6 miles, he and the other three who were left of his party were dragged on shore, quite unable to sustain themselves out of the water, by the retainers of the friendly Rajah Derigbijah Singh. 'Sullivan died some weeks after of cholera; Murphy cannot be found and is believed to be dead.'

Mrs Germon stated:

Friday, 16 October. During this morning Mr De La Fosse, of the 53rd N I, who had survived the massacre at Cawnpore, called and gave us full particulars of the whole affair; poor Mrs J, of the 53rd N I (she and I were brides together in Delhi), died in the entrenchments, and her husband was killed in the boats, but nothing was known about their children. At the commencement of their siege they had only 300 fighting men – soldiers, shopkeepers, and all included – and 400 women, and about 200 children. Mr De La Fosse was in the only boat that got away; they pursued and fired at them, then the boat struck on a sandbank, and they took to the water, and their numbers were eventually reduced to four, who were sheltered by a small Rajah until General Havelock's force arrived at Cawnpore, when they joined it. He said he had to swim and wade six and a half miles after he left the boat.

Chapter 9

House of Sorrow

Early on the morning of 3 July, a cavalry officer rode into Allahabad with intelligence that the garrison at Cawnpore had fallen to the rebels, and later that day two Indian spies confirmed the terrible news. General Henry Havelock had been brought back from the war in Persia to command the British troops.

A flying column consisting of 400 European troops, 300 Sikhs, 120 Irregular Cavalry and two nine-pounder guns was sent out from Allahabad under Major Sydenham George Charles Renaud of the 1st Madras (European) Fusiliers with the purpose of rushing to Wheeler's aid. However, the advance was delayed because Major Renaud continually halted his progress to take punitive measures. Many Indians were hanged at the roadside and their villages were burned. They eventually joined with Havelock's advancing troops, which left Allahabad on 7 July. The column consisted mainly of units of the 78th Highlanders, the 64th Regiment, the 84th Regiment and the 1st Madras Fusiliers, with six artillery guns. However, it was racked by disease and heatstroke, and could only cover about 8 to 10 miles a day on the 100-mile journey.

In Cawnpore the surviving women and children were completely traumatised. They were brought out of the river and collected on the bank. Many of them were wounded with bullets and sword cuts, their dresses were wet and muddy and full of blood. They were ordered to give up whatever valuables they might have hid among their person, before they were led away to the Savada Kothi. This was a large house painted yellow in the civil lines that belonged to the Nana.

As they made their dreary way up from the river, it was recorded by a native:

> I saw that many of the ladies were wounded. Their clothes had blood on them. Two were badly hurt and had their heads bound up with

handkerchiefs. Some were wet, covered with mud and blood; and some had their dresses torn, but all had clothes. I saw one or two children without clothes. There were no men in the party, but only some boys of twelve or thirteen years of age.

Another eyewitness stated:

The ladies clothing was wet and soiled, and some of them were barefoot. Many were wounded. Two of them I observed well, as being wounded in the leg and under the arm.

Among this party were Kate Lindsay and all her three daughters; Jane Dempster and her three sons; Sarah Saunders and her son; and Ellen Probett and her six children. Many more were large families, such as Mrs Reid, the wife of a merchant named George Reid, and Mrs Gilpin, who each had five children, and five members of the Fitzgerald family.

Already in captivity were Rose Greenway and her six children, and Mrs Jacobi and her three children. There were also five male prisoners kept in a separate room; there were three men who had been captured as fugitives from Fatehgarh – Colonel Goldie, Colonel Smith, and Robert Thornhill; along with Edward Greenway and his fourteen-year-old son, Thomas. The wives and families of all four men were also already being held as hostages, along with several more fugitives from Fatehgarh, including Mrs Reen and her seven children, and six members of the Tucker family.

Nana Sahib had placed them all in the hands of a tall, harsh-minded local courtesan from his palace named Begum Hussaini Khanum, who superintended a party of sweepers. She was in her late twenties, but the life she had led had caused a few grey hairs. On or just before 3 July they were all transferred to her quarters in the Bibighar – 'The House of Ladies' – a smaller building with a paved courtyard in the cantonment's magistrate's compound north of the canal, between the city and the river. 'It comprised two principal rooms, each twenty feet by ten; certain windowless closets intended for the use of native domestics; and an open court some fifteen yards square.' The house had the name prior to the rebellion, and had apparently been built by a European for secret rendezvous with his Indian mistress.

Several reports had brought to light the fact that women had been raped under similar circumstances, and it has been suggested that their dreadful condition, unsanitary state and smell, brought about by malnutrition and disease was such that these emaciated women were too physically revolting to touch. It is more likely that the risk of catching disease was the main reason why they were not defiled by their captors.

Each day the Begum selected two women to go to another building to do the menial task of making corn for chipatis, and they were fed on these cakes of unleavened dough and lentil porridge dished up in earthen bowls. 'There was some talk of meat on a Sunday, but this never happened, although on one occasion the children were given a little milk.'

The native head bearer of Colonel Williams tried to get into the house to check on the condition of Georgiana Williams. The sentries would not allow him in, but he witnessed the captives being given some food, which he described as 'native bread and milk'. He remonstrated with a sentry who had also served under Colonel Williams to try to get them something more like the nutritional food they had been used to. The sentry gave him eight annas (twelve pence) to go to the bazaar to buy some sweetmeats. On his return, Georgiana Williams and a married lady came into the veranda and he gave them the sweetmeats. Georgiana repeated her mother's request for him to go to her brother, but when some of the other women came out into the veranda the sentries turned the native out. Another native looked over the wall of the compound and witnessed the women washing their own dirty linen; another labour they were not used to.

Poor sanitary conditions and drinking bad water caused dysentery and cholera to break out, and among the eighteen women who died during the eight days from the 7 to 15 July were Alice Lindsay, who died on 9 July; Ann Fraser is reported to have died of fever on 10 July; and Kate Lindsay died on 12 July. Seven children and a nurse also succumbed to the conditions.

The Nana initially intended to use the captives to bargain with the British, and he became concerned that if they all died he would have nobody to bargain with, so he ordered that each evening they should be herded onto the veranda for some fresh air.

Drummer John Fitchett of the 6th Bengal Native Infantry stated 'On 15 July news came that General Henry Havelock's troops were ruthlessly brushing all opposition aside and were nearing the city in no mood to be bargained with.'

The captives were then seen in a different light and would become witnesses to the atrocities the Nana and his men had already committed. He held a meeting to decide what to do and it was decided that they should all be killed. The news went rapidly through the town, and the men of the 6th Bengal Native Infantry, who had mutinied at Allahabad on 6 June, entered the enclosure with the intention to steal any valuables they could get their hands on. When the Nana heard of this he was enraged, and he sent down a body of sowars with strict orders to surround the house and permit no one to enter but the executioners.

Shortly after 4.30 on the afternoon of Wednesday 15 July some of the Nana's people went across to the house and asked Colonel Goldie, Colonel Smith, Robert Thornhill and Edward and Thomas Greenway to go with them to see Brigadier Jeekin. Some ladies pushed forward out of the doorway and craned their necks to watch the course that the solemn party took, probably Mary Goldie, Mary Smith and Mary Thornhill, but they were pushed back by the sentries. As the unsuspecting men walked quietly along the road in the direction they were told to go they asked where they were going, and were told that they had been sent for on some personal concern.

However, all around was a deep throng of spectators, the foremost rows seated on the ground, so that those behind could see, while others occupied places on the wall of the enclosure, like a small amphitheatre. As they approached the gate leading into the road they saw the Nana lounging beneath a spreading lime tree, the gold lace of his turban glittering in the sunshine. Also there were Jwala Pershad, Tantia Topi, Azimullah and Bala Rao, 'the twinges of whose shoulder-blade heightened his avidity for the coming show'.

When this collection of leaders was noticed by the captives, they realised they were lambs going to their slaughter and their lips were seen to move as if in prayer. As the defenceless men reached the gate close to the Assembly Rooms they were suddenly attacked from behind by a squad of sepoys and cut down and murdered on the spot. Their bodies were thrown on to the grass that bordered the highway, and became the sport of a mocking rabble.

No doubt the sound of firing could be heard at the Bibighar, and to add to the dreadful foreboding and heartbreak of the captives, about half an hour after this the Begum heartlessly informed them that the Nana had decided to have them killed. One of the ladies went up to the native officer who commanded the guard and told him that she had learned they were all to die, but he assured her that if that was so he would have heard something about it; and as he had not she had no cause for concern.

A soldier said to the Begum 'Your orders will not be obeyed. Who are you that you should give orders?' Upon this the Begum went into a rage and hurried off to tell the Nana what had been said. During her absence the sepoys discussed the matter and resolved that they would never lift their weapons against the prisoners. One of them afterwards confessed to a friend that his own motive for so deciding was anxiety to stand well with the British when they got back to Cawnpore.

On her return, sepoys of the 6th Bengal Native Infantry were ordered to fall in, and six of them were told to advance and shoot the captives. They shouted to the women to come out into the courtyard, but they refused and while some ran into the side rooms to hide, others gripped hold of the stone pillars with their children huddled around them, as the senior women among them ripped off strips from their clothing and tied the handles of the doors together to try to keep them out.

The sepoys are said to have been sickened by the task they were asked to do, and that they discharged their muskets through the windows at the ceiling of the apartments, and on hearing the screams of anguish from within they refused to do any more. However, according to some eyewitnesses there were no gunshot marks on the ceiling, only on the walls and pillars, so it seems likely that some of the victims were killed and wounded.

The Begum became angry again, called the sepoys cowards for not finishing the task, and stormed away. She soon returned with five men, some of whom were carrying sabres, and two carried butcher's cleavers. These include a man called Sarvur Khan, wearing the red uniform of the Nana's bodyguard, who is reported to have been her lover, and 'said to be an Afghan – a short stout man with fair hair'. A bystander remarked that he had hair on his hands.

The other four wore dirty white overalls. Two were Hindu peasants: one thirty-five years of age, fair and tall, with a long mustachio, but flat-faced and wall-eyed, another considerably his senior, short, and of a sallow complexion. Two were butchers by calling, portly strapping fellows, both well on in life. The larger of the two was disfigured by traces of smallpox. They must have been Mohammedans, as no Hindu could adopt a trade that obliged him to spill the blood of a cow.

The five men tried to enter the building, but at first their progress was halted by the doors being fastened together. They cut at the doors, and as they broke through the woman who had asked the officer of their fate was standing in the doorway. One of the suspected murderers later stated that he struck a woman with his sword, which bent, and he then felt pity, and did not again strike. With her were the native doctor, and two Hindu ayals (servants). It would seem they had bravely tried to confront the assailants, perhaps trying in vain to beg for their mercy, and they must have been the first victims of cold steel. That much of the atrocity could be seen from the veranda, but all else was concealed amidst the interior gloom. Shrieks and scuffling could be heard by those outside, including Drummer Fitchett, who stated 'I heard fearful shrieks, which lasted half an hour or more. I did not see any of the women or children try to escape.' This was probably because they knew that there was nowhere for them to go for salvation.

It would have been gloomy inside the main rooms but not dark. As most of the others cowered in terror trying to avoid the slashes and swipes, Mrs Jacobi is said to have tried to defend her three children, Henry, Hugh and Lucy, during which time she knocked one of the assailants to the ground. Her actions angered the murderers and it was stated that she was tied to a post and had her throat cut for daring to defend herself. It is likely that women such as Ellen Probett, Sarah Saunders and Bridget Widdowson would have put up some kind of resistance, even in their demoralised and weakened state.

Sarvur Khan soon emerged with his sword broken off at the hilt. He got another from the Nana's house and a few minutes after appeared again on the same errand. The third blade was either of better temper; or perhaps the worst of the work was already over. As it started to get dark, the men came out and locked up the house for the night. Then the screams ceased, but the groans lasted till morning. Jessie Seppings, still nursing her wound, seems to have managed to hide with her two sons somewhere in the gloom among the rest of the mangled corpses. One of the boys was still clutching the wooden toy for comfort.

Evidence of severe cruelty was found later; one child had been put on a hook dangling by its chin and left there to die in agony. One can only hope that the child's mother was already dead.

At about eight o'clock, three hours after the sun came up, the five returned to the scene of their Devil's work. They were attended by four or five sweepers who lived in the compound. A great crowd began to gather, all standing along the walls of the compound looking on. 'They were principally city people and villagers, and there were also sepoys.'

The murderers and their assistants proceeded to transfer the contents of the house to a dry well situated behind some trees that grew nearby. It is believed that they were supposed to throw the bodies into the Ganges, but there were so many victims that they decided on the well. An eyewitness to the whole sordid affair stated:

> The bodies were dragged out, most of them by the hair of the head. Those who had clothes worth taking were stripped. Some of the women were alive. I cannot say how many: but three could speak. They prayed for the sake of God that an end might be put to their sufferings. I remarked one very stout woman, a half-caste [possibly Mary Goldie], who was severely wounded in both arms, who entreated to be killed. She and two or three others were placed against the bank of the cut by which bullocks go down in drawing water. The dead were first thrown in.
>
> Three fair-haired boys were still alive. The eldest, I think, must have been six or seven, and the youngest five years. They ran crying helplessly around the well carrying toys for comfort, but with nowhere to go for safety, and there was none to save them. No; none said a word, or tried to save them.

Two of these poor children were almost certainly John and Edward Seppings.

At length the smallest of them made a desperate attempt to get away. The little thing had been frightened past bearing by the murder of one of the surviving ladies – probably Jessie Seppings. He thus attracted the attention of a native, who flung him and his companions down the well. One witness is of the opinion that the man first took the trouble to kill the children. Others think not. Drummer Fitchett said he saw the youngest of them thrown down the well by one of the sweepers, and he believed that the rest of the survivors were thrown into the well alive. 'The corpses of the gentlemen must have been committed to the same receptacle: for a townsman who looked over the brink fancied that there was "a Sahib uppermost".' These may have been the bodies of the men who had been killed on the previous evening, and thrown there to hide the evidence of their murder too, or to keep the victims who were still alive from getting out, as otherwise they would probably have been dumped in the river.

These disgraceful events happened almost under the shadow of the church tower. Long before noon on 16 July there were no living Europeans in Cawnpore other than those suffocating under the heap of mangled butchered corpses in the well; many of which are said to have been cut up so they could fit.

The relieving force that arrived on 17 July found a note in the doctor's house on which was written most of the names of the victims.

The house of horrors was covered in human gore. The floors and mats were saturated and ankle-deep in blood, and the blood-spattered walls were scored with sword cuts: not high up, as where soldiers have fought; but low down, and about the corners, as if the victims had crouched to avoid a blow. Strips of dresses, vainly tied round the handles of the doors, signified the contrivance to which feminine despair had resorted as a means of keeping out the murderers. Broken combs were there, the frills of children's trousers, torn cuffs and pinafores, little round hats, one or two shoes with burst latchets, and one or two daguerreotype–photo cases with cracked glasses. An officer picked up a few curls, preserved in a bit of cardboard, and marked 'Ned's hair, with love', but around were strewn locks, some near a yard in length, that had not been cut as keepsakes.

An officer wrote:

I picked up a mutilated prayer book. It had lost the cover, but on the fly-leaf is written, 'For dearest Mamma, from her affectionate Louis, June 1845'. It appeared to have been opened on page 36, in the Litany, where I have but little doubt that those poor creatures sought and found consolation, in that beautiful supplication. It is here sprinkled with blood. The book has lost some pages at the end, and terminates with the forty-seventh psalm, in which David thanks the Almighty for his victory over his enemies and a saving mercy.

Two pieces of paper were also found, one being written in an unknown hand:

We went into the barracks on 21 May. The 2nd Cavalry broke out at two o'clock on the morning of 5 June, and the other regiments went off during the day. The next morning, while we were sitting in front of our barracks a twenty-four pounder came flying along and hit the entrenchment, and from that day the firing went on until 25 June, when the enemy sent a treaty, which the general agreed to, and on 27 we all left the B [barracks] to go down to A [Allahabad] in boats. When we got to the river the enemy began firing on us, killing all the gentlemen, and some of the ladies, set fire to the boats. Some were drowned, and we were taken prisoner, taken to a house and put all in one room.

On the other piece of paper, Caroline Lindsay had kept an account of the killed and wounded in a single family (see Appendix I).

The first people to enter the Bibighar discovered a book entitled *Preparation for Death*, and a Bible, which must have travelled in Major Vibart's barge down to Nuzzufgur and back to Cawnpore, and almost certainly belonged to the Blair family, because on the flyleaf was written 'For darling Mamma, from her affectionate daughter Isabella Blair.' (see Appendix I)

Sergeant William Forbes-Mitchell of the 93rd Highlanders was stationed in Cawnpore in September 1857, and stated:

The first place the party reached was General Wheeler's so-called entrenchment, the ramparts of which, at the highest place did not exceed four feet, and were so thin that at the top they could not have been bullet-proof. The entrenchment and the barracks inside of it were complete ruins, and the only wonder about it was how the small force could have held out so long. In the rooms of the buildings were still lying strewn about the remains of articles of women's and children's clothing, broken toys, torn pictures, books, pieces of music, etc.

He also found some writing on the walls but did not comment on what was written. He found a New Testament written in Gaelic without a name in it, and picked it up to keep as a relic. 'All the blank pages had been torn out, most probably used as gun wadding during the most desperate days of the siege.' He thought the Bible belonged to a Scottish Highlander, but it may well have belonged to the Irish Chaplain Montcrieff.

On a visit to the Sati Chaura Ghat he discovered '... many skeletons, etc, lying about unburied among the bushes.'

He then went to see the Bibighar slaughter house, and witnessed: '... the floors of the room were still covered in congealed blood, littered with trampled, torn dresses of women and children, shoes, slippers, and locks of long hair, many of which had evidently been severed from the living scalps by sword-cuts ...'

In one of the rooms he found evidence of hideous cruelty. An iron hook covered with dried blood, which was fixed into the wall about 6ft from the floor. On the whitewashed walls at the height of the hook were the blood-stained handprints of a child and below it the same child's bloody footprints. It seemed that the child had been hung there by the chin facing the wall, where it must have struggled until death brought relief.

Major George Bingham of the 64th Regiment stated:

The place was literally running ankle deep in blood, ladies' hair torn from their heads was lying about the floor; poor little children's shoes lying here and there, gowns, frocks and bonnets belonging to these poor creatures scattered everywhere. But to crown all horrors, after they had been killed, and even some alive, all were thrown down a deep well in the compound. I looked down and saw them lying in heaps. I very much fear there are some of my friends included in this most atrocious fiendish of murders.

Chapter 10

'Remember Cawnpore!'

One thing that was certain was the British forces that were coming to avenge their brethren would be a courageous army led by ruthless and determined commanders, and the Amirs of Sind had suffered a good example of this. On his way to the conquest of the region, Sir Charles Napier won a particularly bloody battle near the main town of Hyderabad on 17 February 1843. The Amirs asked Napier on what terms he was prepared to accept their surrender. Napier told them 'Life and nothing more. And I want your decision before twelve o'clock, as I shall by that time have buried my dead, and given my soldiers their breakfasts.'

One by one the Amirs gave in, recognising in Napier a man as ruthless as themselves. 'Come in and submit,' he told them, and if they chose not to he promised fire and sword. To one 'whose barbarian pride would not bend', he sent a simple chilling message 'Come alone and make your submission, or I will in a week tear you from the midst of your tribe and hang you.'

After the annexation of Scinde he was appointed governor of the new province, and his methods did not change. He gave swords back to the chiefs with the threat 'Take back your sword. You have used it with honour against me, and I esteem a brave enemy. But if forgetful of this voluntary submission you draw it again in opposition to my government, I will tear it from you and kill you like a dog.'

His despatch to Lord Ellenborough after his victory consisted of one emphatic word: *Peccavi* – 'I have sinned' – Scinde.

As governor he abolished slavery and the practice of 'suttee', when widows were burned alive on the pyres of their husbands. When complaints were made on the grounds that he was interfering with their customs, Napier responded 'My nation has also a custom. When men burn women alive we hang them. My carpenters shall therefore erect gibbets on which to hang all concerned when the widow is consumed. Let us all act to our national customs.' It is hardly surprising that he came to be known as 'Satan's brother.'

British retribution was indeed dreadful.

The recapture of Cawnpore would be the first stage in the plan to relieve the residency at Lucknow, and the dreadful events that happened there enraged every British soldier bearing arms and fuelled a great desire for revenge. General Neill vowed that he would punish most fiercely the people who had been responsible for the murders. On 25 July he issued an order that every captured rebel, whether proved guilty or not, should be punished – even for standing back and allowing it to happen. He decided that every drop of British blood should be cleared up and wiped out by those responsible for the atrocity, and therefore he was to have his caste defiled by having to kneel down and lick clean a square foot of the floor of the murder scene. The Highlanders, many becoming hysterical with rage and pity, took an oath that for every one of those murdered 100 of the enemy should die. Captain Garnet Wolseley, who later rose to the highest ranks of the British army, admitted that his sword was thirsty for revenge and that he would have 'Blood for blood, not drop for drop, but barrels and barrels of the filth which flows in these niggers' veins for every drop of blood which marked the floors and walls of that fearful house.'

One soldier, who had his opinions poisoned by stories of the atrocities, reported 'I seed two Moors (Indians) talking in a cart. Presently I heard one of 'em say "Cawnpore". I knowed what that meant: so I fetched Tom Walker, and he heard 'em say "Cawnpore", and he knowed what that meant. So we polished 'em both off.'

Indiscriminate lynchings were carried out by 'volunteer hanging parties'. However, hanging was considered too compassionate for mutineers. When the facilities were available, it was usual to perform the hideous task of blasting them from guns. This was terrible for the beholder who was next in line to suffer the same punishment. The victim would be escorted to the parade ground while the regimental band played music. He was them strapped to the muzzle of one of the big guns, and as the band became silent the fuse was lit and with a flash and a roar the unfortunate victim's body would produce an obscene shower of blood and guts cascading over all the onlookers.

It seems that each man who carried out the murders in the Bibighar was given one rupee for every life he took, and most of them spent it on betel nut, a vine leaf-based stimulant that had been chewed by most Indians for thousands of years. Regular use stains the gums and teeth a deep red colour. A shopkeeper in Ooghoo later stated that two of the murderers were among a party of men who had escaped from Cawnpore and threatened to cut off his head if he did not give them good-quality betel leaf for a very low price:

> They said that they had shown no pity to the ladies and children whom they had just murdered, and who clung to their feet, and that they would have no pity upon me. I heard their companions ask the two men how many ladies they had killed. They replied that they had murdered twenty-one ladies and children, and had received a reward of twenty-one rupees.

Souracun Begum was a thirty-five-year-old peasant with a defect in his eye who lived in Ooghoo. It was well-known in the town that he was one of the murderers, and he sometimes even admitted that he was involved. He stated that he 'struck a lady with such force that the weapon bent. Then he felt pity and did not strike again.' On telling this story some time later he produced the bent sword he said he used. He said that he earned twenty-one rupees, which he spent on betel leaves.

An individual named Gungoo Mehter was tried for the murder of many of the women and children in the Bibighar. He was convicted and hanged on 8 September 1857.

It was Brigadier Jwala Prasad who gave General Wheeler his personal guarantee that no harm would come to any of the defenders of the entrenchment if they surrendered. And yet he would play an instrumental role in directing the withering fire on the boats at Sati Chaura when the massacre was ordered. He was captured in 1859 and hanged from a tree at the scene of the atrocity at what had then become known as Massacre Ghat.

The British had little respect for the abilities of the rebel leaders, except Tantia Tope. They considered him to be a capable opponent. An officer of the 17th Lancers stated:

The marvellous activity, fertility of resource and swiftness of action of the blood-stained instrument of the massacre of Cawnpore, made him a foeman worthy even of Englishmen's steel ... ubiquity was in the man. He had a wonderful genius for wild warfare, and extraordinary skill in the employment of his knowledge of the locality, and he swept with strange facility across vast tracts of country to the surprise of his enemies ... As is well-known, he paid the forfeit of his life for his sanguinary deeds; but we cannot withhold our tribute of admiration from a man who showed such military genius in guerrilla warfare, and eluded us so resolutely and so long.

Tantia Tope later arranged the defence of Bithur, which posed a difficult trial for Havelock and his troops, and he repelled Windham at Cawnpore on 28 November. However, he was defeated by Colin Campbell at the decisive battle of Cawnpore on 6 December, thus ending the campaign in the Doab, and bringing about the capture of Fatehgarh.

He progressed with the Gwalior contingent, and came to the relief of Rani Lakshmibai of Jhansi, with whom he seized the city of Gwalior. However, he was twice defeated by British East India troops under Hugh Rose in June 1858, after which he abandoned the campaign and took to fighting as a guerrilla in the jungle of Rajputana. He was reduced in support and loyalty as his followers dispersed, finally left with just one friend named Man Singh. Man Singh betrayed him to the Rajah of Nawar, who had been persuaded to rehabilitate his reputation with the British and betray the rebel leader. On being handed over to Major Maude, and probably being well aware that he would be executed whatever he might say, he admitted to all the charges brought before him, saying that he was answerable only to his master, the Peshwa. He was escorted to the gallows at Shivpuri on 18 April 1859 by a squadron of the 17th Lancers, which included a number of men who had ridden in the Charge of the Light Brigade.

An air of mystery surrounds the death of the Rani of Jhansi, but she was killed on 17 June 1858, probably as the 8th Hussars, another unit that had charged with the Light Brigade at Balaclava, were in the process of attacking her forces during the taking of the fort at Gwalior.

Begum Hazrat Mahal was forced to retreat to Nepal in 1858, where she was initially refused asylum by the Rana prime minister, Jang Bahadur, but she was eventually allowed to stay. She spent the remaining years of her life there, passing away in Kathmandu on 7 April 1879. She was buried in the grounds of the Jama Musjid. On the occasion of Queen Victoria's Golden Jubilee in 1887 the British Government pardoned the Rani of Oudh and he was allowed to return home. Despite being considered an icon of what some consider to have been India's first freedom struggle, Hazrat Mahal's mausoleum fell into a neglected state, and she was forgotten at the centenary of the First War of Independence held in Uttar Pradesh, becoming a lost hero in the pages of Indian history. However, the Government of India issued fifteen million commemorative stamps in honour of the Begum on 10 May 1984.

Nana Sahib, Bala Rao, Teeka Singh and Azimullah Khan were said to have been driven into the inhospitable border country of the Nepalese Terai wetlands by the British late in 1859, where they are believed to have died of fever. Some sources suggest that Azimullah escaped to live with a woman named Clayton. The Nana Sahib became the most wanted man in the British Empire, and until long after the rebellion there were reported sightings of him, the last said to have been at Gujarat in 1895 when a young British officer detained an elderly Sadhu and cabled Calcutta: 'Have arrested the Nana Sahib. Wire instructions.' Not wishing to rake up the past in an India that had moved on, the reply from Calcutta came: 'Release at once.'

However, the following report appeared in several newspapers in early March 1895: NANA SAHIB: It will be recollected that some months ago a wire was received that this notorious butcher of Cawnpore had been captured and would have justice meted out to him. The said capture has only been another mistake, as will be seen by the following:

There has been a good deal of excitement in India over the supposed arrest of the notorious Nana Sahib. A member of the Kaithiawar Agency Police discovered him in a temple some 30 miles out of Rajcote (Gujarat) not long ago. He was disguised as a fakir, but the features tallied so closely with those given in the description of Nana Sahib circulated by Government that the policeman had the man stripped of his clothing and closely examined. There were found on his body certain peculiar marks that were known to be on the body of the real Nana Sahib.

Nana at first seemed terribly scared, and shouted, 'Saheb, mhaf karo, mfaf karo!' (Hindu for Saheb, please, forgive me!) – and also stated that he would tell everything. But just, however, as he was about to make a statement he seemed to recollect his position, and decided to keep a still tongue.

He was for several weeks in the charge of the police, and several witnesses from Cawnpore were brought down to identify him. One of the men, who is supposed to have served under the Nana, was about to say that he identified the fakir when he suddenly stopped himself and disowned all knowledge of the old man. In this he was followed by the other witnesses, and so, under the circumstances, the police have had to allow the supposed Nana to return to his temple and his asceticism.

Nana Sahib found a place in Madame Tussauds' Chamber of Horrors, where it written that he '… died the coward's death, despised and forsaken.' The *Dictionary of National Biography* is correct in its statement concerning the Nana Sahib '… whose barbarous cruelty and treachery have never been forgotten', and he is 'marked with an abiding stigma'.

It is interesting to note that William Urwick, after his visit to Cawnpore, asserted:

One thinks of Cawnpore with a shudder, and leaves it with a sigh. The fact, however, must be recorded whenever the sad story is told that the most careful Government investigations failed to discover a single case on the part of the sepoys of mutilations before death or of torture, or of the dishonour of women during the Indian Mutiny.

During the inquest into the condition of the woman prisoners, Queen Victoria ventured to know of their virtue, and asked if they had been forcibly defiled by the Mutineers, because she was aware that the rape of European women was common in similar circumstances. The Queen, although outraged, was said to be comforted by the news that no such atrocity had been performed.

Ironically, while much of the fighting during the mutiny was carried out with the point of the bayonet and sword, the rifle that the rebels had rejected was a major factor in their downfall. While the rebels retained the clumsy old muzzle-loading 'Brown Bess', and continued to have to fumble with separate packets of bullets and gunpowder to charge their weapons, the British were able to take advantage of their much more efficient new Enfield rifles, which were loaded with ammunition that combined the bullet with gunpowder in one single cartridge. The British soldiers were well-drilled in the use of the new rifle, especially those who arrived in India as reinforcements, and the weapon was also far more accurate.

Chapter 11

Commemoration

It is thought that four English women and three others of mixed parentage were carried off by men of the 2nd Cavalry. The Nana later remonstrated with them and ordered that all seven should be returned without delay. They all are said to have obeyed his command, except a young sowar named Nazim Ali Khan. However, Amy Horne and a fourteen-year-old girl named Amelia Spiers were also taken away from the ghat. Miss Spiers is not listed as being among the victims in the Bibighar, and she was never heard of again. She was the daughter of Band-Sergeant David Spiers of the 53rd Bengal Native Infantry and his wife, Hannah. Hannah and her other children, Eliza, Isabella, Matilda and Fred, are believed to have survived.

Margaret (Ulrica) Wheeler survived the massacre at the ghat, having been saved from death by Ali Khan. Amy Horne stated that she was near Ulrica on the bank of the river where their captors had put them out of danger, until they were able to carry them off. Soon afterwards a story circulated that she had killed the sowar and several members of his family, and in a 'death before dishonour' act she then threw herself down a well to commit suicide and protect her virtue. This story is said to have been circulated to satisfy the moral principles of the British imperial elite, and to make the event 'real' an engraving depicting her heroic deed was produced at the time. However, this story was later discredited.

Ulrica is believed to have formed a bond with the sowar and eventually married him. Being of mixed race, she was able to live undetected in the Indian section of Cawnpore, and she decided not to disclose to anyone that she was still alive, or her whereabouts, because she did not want her husband to get into trouble. In 1907 a priest (some accounts say a female missionary) in Cawnpore was attending a Eurasian woman lying on her death bed when she confessed that she was Margaret Wheeler, and most historians of the subject tend to agree that this was her true fate. One item of evidence of this came from an officer's wife who lived in Cawnpore and knew Ulrica before the rebellion. She stated that after the mutiny she was contacted by Ulrica through a servant, and she made regular visits to her bungalow, where she tried on her friend's western clothes and admired herself in a mirror.

Amy Horne was carried off by a sowar of the 2nd Native Cavalry and secreted in a hut near the Savada Kothi, after which she was kept by him for ten months. On 7 April 1858, she arrived at the home of Nicholas Flouest, her mother's brother. She was dressed in native clothes and her English was not good, so it took her some time to prove her identity. Eventually, she was accepted, and on the last day of the month she wrote a letter to the Governor's secretary claiming a compensation – which was turned down.

Accounts differ as to whether she married under the sowar's duress during her captivity. If she did it must be assumed it was later annulled because on 20 September 1858 she married William Bennett, a railway worker, who was said to be twice Amy's age. They had one son and two daughters before William died in 1877. The children were Amy Grob (1859–1926); William Grob (1860–1912); and Ethel Grob (born on 5 February 1862 in Calcutta).

Describing herself as a 'pauper', in later life she lived in Howrah, 'a dreary suburb of Calcutta', and supported her family by giving piano lessons. She left several different accounts of her experiences, and in 1913 she published a final revised account in which she stated that her 'flesh crept at the recollection of the horrors I had gone through, which made me live my sufferings over again'. She died in 1921.

The first news of the terrible fate of Lieutenant Saunders appears to have been reported by an NCO of the 84th Regiment who arrived at Cawnpore with Havelock's column. In a letter home, published in the *Times* on 19 September 1857, he wrote:

At Cawnpore, a cook-boy, who was with G Company by some means escaped; being a Bengalee of course he could mix with the remainder of his class without detection. He is but a lad; he told us that Mr Saunders was nailed down, hands, feet, and knees; and that these barbarians the first day cut off his feet and ears and nose, and so left him until the next day when some other pieces were cut off him, and he died. He had killed six men, and would have shot Nena [sic] Sahib also, that terrible ruffian, but his revolver did not go off.

The following is an extract of a letter from Lance-Corporal David Tracey of the 84th Regiment, written to a comrade in Dum Dum:

Lieutenant Saunders (H.M. 84th) was brought before the Rajah Sanna Saheb. He pulled out his revolver, shot dead five of the guard, and they crucified him to the ground. The whole of the cavalry charged past, and every one of them had a cut at him; he was cut to pieces by the whole of them.

The news of the murder of Kate Lindsay and her family was sent home to her sister, Mary, by Captain William Moorsom of the 52nd (Oxfordshire) Light Infantry, who arrived at Cawnpore with the relief column and was a friend of Kate. Mary had considerable difficulty in proving that her three orphaned nephews were entitled to the Bengal Military Orphans' Fund. One of the orphans was William Lindsay, who had been born in Benares on 3 August 1847. He went on to play cricket for England, and was a full-back for the England football team. As a member of the celebrated Wanderers FC, he won the Football Association Challenge Cup winners' medals three years running from 1876 to 1878.

Robert Thornhill's brother, John Bensley, was assistant-commissioner at Lucknow. He had been married to General Havelock's niece, Mary, for only a year, and had an infant child. When Havelock's troops were approaching Lucknow he volunteered to go out and guide them through the city. He was mortally wounded on 27 September 1857 while trying to save a number of men, including Havelock's eldest son, at the Lucknow Residency.

Mark Bensley Thornhill had been a deputy collector at Cawnpore, and in 1857 he was a magistrate at Muttra. He managed to get out of the area by posing as a Muslim woman in order to make his escape. He published his memoir in 1884 and died in 1891.

His son, George John Thornhill (1842–1915), emigrated to Otago in New Zealand in 1861 and engaged in sheep farming. He was joined by his brother, Edward Augustus, in 1867. Edward died at Southlands, New Zealand, in 1922.

Ann Fraser's mother died in 1870, and Colonel Thomas Charge Wray of the 2nd Battalion, Royal Irish Regiment, served in New Zealand during the latter stages of the Maori Wars in 1866 and in Egypt in 1884.

Lieutenant-General McCausland spent forty-three years of his life serving in India, before he returned to Cheltenham, where he died at Melrose Villa on 23 July 1879. His wife, Emma, died on 28 July 1889 in England.

In his book *A Pictorial Record of the Cawnpore Massacre*, Lieutenant Charles Wade Crump of the Madras Artillery, who was with the first wave of troops under General Havelock that marched to the relief of Lucknow, produced three colour lithographs, including one of the interior of the Bibighar as he saw it on site at the time. It was entitled *The Chamber of Blood* and became the template for all future sketches of the Bibighar interior. Lieutenant Crump was killed in action at Lucknow in September 1857. In a letter to his mother, another witness on site stated that some writings on the walls, such as 'countrymen revenge' were put there by British soldiers and not by the women.

The British dismantled the Bibighar house after the rebellion was crushed, and the area around it was cleared of trees. They raised an iron memorial railing and a cross at the site of the well, and then the native inhabitants of Cawnpore were forced to pay a fine of £30,000 for the creation of a permanent memorial; this was partial punishment for not coming to the aid of the women and children in the Bibighar. *The Angel of the Resurrection* was completed in 1865, and came to be the most visited historical site in British India, even more so than the Taj Mahal at Agra.

The chief proponents and private funders were Charlotte, Countess Canning (1817–61), wife of the first Viceroy of India, Earl Canning; and Louisa Anne Beresford (1818–91), wife of the 3rd Marquess of Waterford. Louisa asked her childhood friend, Baron Carlo Marochetti, to produce some models. Following the Countess's death, Earl Canning took over the commission, and after rejecting a number of designs from various sculptors he eventually accepted a version of Marochetti's Crimean War memorial at Scutari in Turkey.

The mournful seraph figure is an angel holding two branches of palm fronds across her chest, and standing on a pedestal marking the site of the well. It originally had an octagonal marble gothic screen around it, which had been designed by Henry Yule in 1865, above the entrance of which were inscribed the words: 'These are they which came out of great tribulation', and another around it read: 'Sacred to the perpetual memory of a great company of Christian people, chiefly women and children, who near this spot were cruelly massacred and cast into the well below on the 15th day of July, 1857.' A memorial garden was set out around the monument, and a large landscaped park of 30 acres was laid out. For many years the memorial garden was banned to all Indians without a special pass, and colonial visitors were expected to slow their carriages as a mark of respect as they passed the monument.

Despite assurances otherwise, the memorial received some damage during the Independence celebrations of 1947 and was later moved from its original site over the well to a garden at the side of All Souls Church which the British had erected in memory of the victims. It was designed in Gothic red brick by Walter Granville, who was the architect of the East Bengal Railway, and was completed in 1875.

The site of the well is now in the Nana Rao Park, where the remains of a circular ridge of it can still be seen. A bust of Tantia Tope, which could have been sited somewhere else in the park, has been placed close to the well. A descendant of some of the victims who visited the site in 2017 commented: 'They are doing some earth works, and among the rubble they have dug up are fragments of the gothic screen which must have been left when the memorial was removed after independence. Only a brown eighteen metre circle of concrete covers the well and where the memorial stood.' At one time no games or amusements were allowed in the park, but now, as the visitor concludes 'Kids play cricket here on top of the grave every day. They don't seem to have a clue what's under their feet. To my mind, the placing of a bust of Tantia Tope overlooking the well shows the same insensitivity as if they erected a statue of Hitler at the gates of Auschwitz-Birkenau.'

The church contains fourteen memorial tablets with the known names of the victims. It is now known as the Kanpur Memorial Church. The inscriptions begin 'To the Glory of God and in memory of more than a thousand Christian people who met their deaths hard by between 6th June and 15th July 1857. These tablets are placed in this the Memorial Church, All Souls, Cawnpore by the Government, N W Provinces.'

Nearby a stone tablet states 'In three graves within this enclosure lie the remains of Major Edward Vibart, 2nd Bengal Light Cavalry, and about seventy officers and soldiers who, after escaping from the massacre at Cawnpore on the 27th June 1857 were captured by the rebels at Sheorajpoor, and murdered on the 1st July. These remains were originally interred within the compound of Sivada House and were removed to this place in April 1861.'

A marble memorial tablet was placed in Cawnpore church dedicated to 'E G Chalwin, 2nd Light Cavalry, and his wife Louisa: Who both perished during the Siege of Cawnpore in July 1857. These are they which came out of great tribulation.'

Another individual memorial tablet states 'Sacred to the memory of LIEUT. FREDERICK CORTLAND ANGELO, 16th Grenadiers. B.N.I. Superintendent of the 4th division Ganges Canal, who fell in the Mutiny at Cawnpore on the 27th June 1857 in the 32nd year of his age. "Jesus said I am the resurrection and the life. He that believeth in me, though he were dead, yet shall he live". St John XI 25. This tablet is erected by his sorrowing widow.'

The Angelo family travelled by river from Cawnpore, and during the trip their faithful Indian servants hid them in the bottom of the boat to get them through danger points. They reached Calcutta on 1 July, and Frederick Canning Cortlandt was born on 21 September 1857. Helena had been befriended by Lady Canning, who agreed to be godmother to the new baby. The family sailed for England on RMS *Nile* on 20 November. Frederick was killed in action on 26 March 1880 while serving as a lieutenant with the 31st Punjab Native Infantry (Cortland's) during the defence of the Battye Fort in Afghanistan. Helena died in 1908, and Helena junior became Mrs Richard Whiteway and died at Shottermill in Surrey in 1911. Catherine became known to the family as 'Aunt Kitty'. She died at Hove in Sussex in 1949.

An individual memorial in All Souls Church states 'To the memory of John Robert Mackillop of the Bengal Civil Service, who was killed at Cawnpore on or about the 25th June 1857, in his 31st year. He nobly lost his life when bringing water from the well for the distressed women and children. His death was deeply lamented.'

As Lieutenant-Colonel William Gordon-Alexander of the 93rd Highlanders was on his way to the relief of Lucknow on 3 November 1857, he went to see the Bibighar house, during which he noticed a lock of hair attached to some prickly plants growing at the mouth of the well. He collected the hair and eventually had it mounted on a velvet board inside a glass case. Having already presented a copy of his memoirs to Queen Victoria in 1898, he presented the glass case to the Junior United Services Club in 1901. It is now in the collection of the National Army Museum, along with a child's black shoe, a manicure box, and a paper knife picked up on 25 October 1857 by Sergeants C. Brooks and I. Ronayne of the 9th Lancers (probably two veterans of the Second Anglo–Sikh War named George Charles Brooks and John Ronayne). All four items are believed to have been retrieved from the area around the well.

The collection also includes a brass betel nut box that Lieutenant John Claude Auchinleck of the Royal Artillery took from the Nana's treasury at Bithur on 7 December 1857. It had been hidden in a well along with 2 million rupees and countless precious objects. Lieutenant Auchinleck was the father of Field Marshal, Sir Claude Auchinleck, the commander-in-chief in India from 1943 until 1947. There is also a snuff box containing a lock of Tantia Tope's hair cut from his head after his execution.

The toy carried by the Seppings boys was picked up from the murder scene by Hindus who knew who they were, and it was given to Henry Havelock and his men as they entered Cawnpore. The relic found its way to Jessie's brother, Doctor James Somerville Turnbull in New Zealand, and it has remained with the family ever since. There is a story that the phantoms of two little fair-haired boys had been seen running around the well from time to time during the years following the massacre.

An inscription on a memorial at Futtehghur Churchyard dedicated to the victims states:

Erected by the Government, North-West Provinces, to the memory of the Christian residents of Futtehghur in the year of Our Lord 1857, who perished in the troubles of that period. The bodies of some lie in the well beneath; of others the resting place is unknown; yet not one of them is forgotten before God. The lamb which is in the midst of the throne shall feed them and shall lead them unto living waters, and God shall wipe away all tears from their eyes.

There were two gunners named Sullivan at Cawnpore, Timothy and James, both said to have been killed at the ghat. However, Gunner Sullivan, apparently the 'most intelligent' of the four men who escaped by way of the River Ganges, was appointed to the Ordnance Department by General Neill, but he died of cholera on or before 15 January 1858, apparently in Cawnpore.

It seems he told Thomson and De La Fosse that he had dug up a mass of melted silver from the burned out barracks during the siege and reburied it in the entrenchment. Lieutenant Thomson found the place where it had been buried, but all the silver was gone.

Only Private Murphy survived of the 84th Regiment. He went back to India, where he was appointed caretaker of the Cawnpore Memorial Garden and remained there for a few years guiding tourists around the site each day. In his book of 1891, William Urwick asserted: 'Near the railway station a fine old soldier of Havelock's army, who was in all the fighting of 1857, keeps a hotel, and acts as guide to his visitors. Our guide first led us over Wheeler's Entrenchment, now green and garden-like …'

However, Murphy's experiences haunted him, and the historian Henry Busteed wrote of him:

Poor fellow, he was an inveterate drunkard, and though he got several chances nothing could be done with him. When drunk he would sometimes harangue and protest that Lord Canning ought not to be Viceroy of India while such a man as Mowbray Thomson was to the fore! He was a harmless poor devil ruined by the habit of the British soldier. At last he was remanded to his regiment again as a full private, and a hopeless case. Then I believe he died.

However, he did not die, and he eventually transferred to the 2nd Battalion, 20th Regiment (later the Lancashire Fusiliers). Because of his heavy drinking, his health began to break down. On 15 February 1869, he was a patient in the Royal Victoria Hospital, from where he submitted an application for employment with the Corps of Commissionaires to allow him to 'maintain myself and family with credit'.

In November 1913 various newspapers began to report:

Private Murphy and the Cawnpore Massacre. A quiet little Irishman in a pith helmet and linen jacket, Private Murphy was, some fifty years ago, guardian of the Memorial Gardens in Cawnpore. Anglo–Indians visiting the historical spot would chat to him with interest, for he was one of the very few survivors of Nana Sahib's treacherous massacre of June 26 1857.

Mowbray Thomson was invalided home because of his two wounds and received promotion to brevet-major. He and Lieutenant de la Fosse set sail from Calcutta bound for Suez aboard the SS *Ava* on 10 February 1858. The passengers included women and children refugees from the rebellion, along with Lady Inglis, the wife of Major-General John Inglis, who had commanded the troops at Lucknow. Six nights later the ship struck a rock known as Pigeon Island, situated 15 miles north of Trincomalee in Ceylon and sank, taking with it Mowbray Thomson's notes; Edward Vibart's letters; one of William Howard Russell's despatches for *The Times*; and the journals of Martin Gubbins, a commissioner at Lucknow. The passengers were put into seven ship's boats, and after spending a stressful time for the rest of the night stranded in boats on the open sea they were rescued without loss of life.

On his return to Blighty, Thomson visited Dr Grieg, his old tutor at Walthamstow House, where they lamented on several former pupils who had died during the rebellion, including Lieutenant Angelo. After reading 'many conflicting statements' concerning the siege and massacres at Cawnpore, in 1859 he decided to present his own account of the 'distressing history'. He dedicated the work '… to the memory of the brave men, the patient women, and the helpless innocents of England, more than a thousand in number who perished in the brutal massacre perpetrated upon the garrison at CAWNPORE, during the sepoy revolt of MDCCCLVII.'

At Calcutta, on 26 November 1859, Thomson married Mary Ironside (born on 4 August 1835), who was the daughter of the Reverend William Money (1802–90), and his wife, Julia (formerly Ironside, who died on 22 August 1903); who lived at Lea Marston in Warwickshire. They had five children:

Lieutenant-Colonel Mowbray Townshend Thomson was born at Cawnpore on 10 September 1860, and later served with the 4th Gurkha Rifles. He died at Battle in Sussex in 1931.

Ethel Augusta was born at Cawnpore on 16 November 1861. She died at Bexhill-on-Sea in 1945.

Mary Isabel Jessica Ironside was born at Allahabad on 26 February 1863, and died at Eastbourne in 1944.

Lilias Lee died age nineteen in 1884 (born in about 1865). She is buried at Ford Cemetery in Liverpool.

Kathleen Prendergast was born in India on 13 August 1866. She married the Reverend Ottley and had five children in India. She died at Eastbourne in 1892.

Winifred Ernle was born at Kashmir on 20 November 1867. She died on 10 June 1927, and is buried at Bexhill-on-Sea Cemetery in East Sussex.

At the time of the 1871 census, Mary and the children were living at Rugby in Warwickshire, although the family seems to have settled in the Eastbourne area. Mowbray's mother died at Pembridge Villas on 12 March 1884, and she was buried in the Kensington and Chelsea area.

On returning to India, Thomson was given civilian position as political agent at Manipur, and later became the governor-general's agent for the former King of Oudh, at Garden Reach in Calcutta. He was promoted to colonel on 9 November 1880 and major-general on 2 July 1885, the year he was placed on the retired list. As a man who had seen such suffering, the peace and quiet of the Berkshire countryside attracted him, and at the time of the 1891 census he was living at 73 Stirling Road in Wantage. He was appointed a full general on 1 April 1894, and in 1901 he had settled at 19 Victoria Square, St Giles in Reading, where he remained for the rest of his life.

It seems that he became estranged from his wife, and she does not appear on any of these census records. She is reported to have died on 4 August 1903, and is buried at Ocklynge in Eastbourne. Her headstone states that it was erected by her children, giving no mention of Mowbray, and probate went to Ethel and not Mowbray.

John Sherer dedicated his book, *Cawnpore*, to him in 1910 '… in token of a long friendship.' Sherer was of the opinion that Thomson should have received more recognition for his actions at Cawnpore. Nevertheless, Colonel Thomson was appointed KCIE (Knight Commander of the India Empire) in 1911 in connection with his work during the visit to India of King Edward VII for the Coronation Durbar at Delhi; and he was made a KH (Knight of Hanover) for his distinguished military service.

Sherer also remembered being told a story by a banker who dined with Sir Mowbray in London. When the banker asked 'When you got once more amongst all your countrymen, and the whole terrible thing was over, what on Earth was the first thing you did?' To which the stalwart and daring adventurer replied 'Did? Why I went and reported myself as present and ready for duty!'

Mowbray Thomson died on 25 February 1917, aged eighty-four. He left a large sum of money to Henry Doveton, a retired lieutenant-colonel of the Royal Engineers.

A brass plaque in the Memorial church at Cawnpore dedicated to him states 'To the Memory of General, Sir Mowbray Thomson, KCIE, the last survivor of Nana Sahib's Massacre at Cawnpore on June 6th 1857 – He was at the time a Captain in the 53rd Native Infantry. Born April 1st 1832 – Died Feb. 25th 1917.

Colonel Thomson also wrote in his book:

Four of us escaped the massacre committed by the Nana; of this number one, Private Sullivan, died a few weeks afterwards of cholera; a second, Private Murphy, is, I fear, also dead, as all my endeavours to obtain information of him have failed. I had hoped to induce my friend, Lieutenant de la Fosse, to have contributed some of his recollections to the pages of this work; but the numerous engagements in which he has been occupied, have deprived me of the satisfaction it would have given had he taken part in the narration.

Henry de la Fosse recovered from the ordeal to fight in the relief of Lucknow, for which he received the Indian Mutiny Medal with *Lucknow* and *Relief of Lucknow* clasps. He also recieved the thanks of the governor-general of Lucknow in council for his services there, where an advanced battery bore his name. He was also permitted by the military to add two years further service for Cawnpore and Lucknow. He published a brief account of the siege for *The Times*, but not a full memoir like Thomson and Shepherd, although one of his sons, Sir Claude Fraser de la Fosse (1868–1950) wrote a *History of India* in 1917.

Although it was said that he was 'most emaciated' from the constant effects of fever and dysentery, he returned to India in 1860, and went on active service during the Umbeyla Campaign on the North-West Frontier, being present at the assault on Crag Piquet on 30 October 1863. He was in Colonel Acklom Smith's old command at Fatehgarh for two years, and in 1887 was appointed major-general.

He married Helen Scott (formerly Fraser, born Seroor, India, in 1843) at Bath in March 1863, and they had three sons and four daughters before she died of tuberculosis in Paddington, London, on 22 April 1877. In 1871 he was a major living with his family at Farnborough in Hampshire; in 1881 he was a colonel living with his family at 1 Bute Villas in St Paul's, Hammersmith, London, with his mother, a sister, and three of his children; and in 1891 he was a lodger at 7 Torrington Square, Bloomsbury St George, London, being described as a fifty-five-year-old retired major-general in the Indian Army.

Henry was declared bankrupt in 1898 and is believed to have gone to Jersey to escape his creditors. In 1900 he married Anne Ruddle (formerly Bignell, 1868–1927) who was thirty-five years younger than him, and they lived at 3 Lansdowne Villas in Dicq Road, St Saviour, Jersey. Henry died on 9 February 1905. His descendants spelled the family surname as De La Fosse. A plaque was erected at All Souls Church in Cawnpore, which reads 'To the Memory of General Henry George De La Fosse, CB,

DSO, who, after serving with conspicuous bravery in the beleaguered garrison of Cawnpore, fought with distinguished gallantry in the relief of Lucknow, and later on other fields. Born 24 April 1835, died 10 February 1905.'

Jonah Shepherd returned to the Commissariat Department after the siege and remained with the unit for several months, where he tried to compile a definitive list of all the casualties of the Cawnpore atrocities, during which time he amassed a voluminous file of letters from relatives in the UK. However, the dreadful events he had witnessed and suffered had seriously affected his faculties and his ability to concentrate, and he wrote 'My impaired memory, and loss of power to fix my attention, compelled me often to put aside work that required immediate attention …' Unfortunately, his memory continued to fade.

He was relieved of his duties in the following December and went to live with his brother at Agra. In 1860 he was given an appointment in the Executive Commissariat Office. However, in 1862 he had to take medical leave, 'mental anxiety' being given as one of the reasons for this. During this time he wrote his book about his experiences during the rebellion, *A Personal Narrative of the Outbreak and Massacre at Cawnpore during the Sepoy Revolt of 1857.*

Lord Elgin bestowed a small estate to him in recognition of his service during the rebellion, which he named 'Elgingurh' as a gesture of thanks. He gave all his time to managing the estate but it proved to be a failure. He lost 20 acres of the land to the Oudh and Rohilkland Railway, and in 1873 he was forced to take a job with the company. Three years later he sold the rest of his failing estate.

He revised his *Personal Narrative* in 1879, and in the same year he wrote *The Guilty Men of 1857: England's Great Mission to India,* in which he blamed the uprising on the government's attempts to force Christianity on the India population.

Jonah Shepherd died in 1891 and his descendants believe that he was buried in Lucknow. It seems that the only thing that would not fade from his memory were the tragic events of 1857, and because 'Uncle Jonah' had such bad luck the family would never name a child after him.

Captain Adam Montague Turnbull has his name commemorated on the memorial in the Residency at Lucknow and in All Souls Church in Cawnpore. He was actually stationed at Lucknow and he was the only man of his unit present at Cawnpore during the siege. He may well have been there visiting Jessie Seppings, whose unmarried name was Turnbull and they may have been related. The 13th mutinied at Lucknow on 30 May, and two officers from the unit, Colonel Robert Aitken and Lieutenant William Cubitt, were awarded the Victoria Cross for gallantry in and around the city.

Another story concerns Captain Thomas Waterman of the 13th, who, after days of being on constant alert, fell asleep while the city was being evacuated by Havelock's force. When he woke up he found that the city had been taken over by the rebels and he had to make a mad dash to freedom through the squalid sewage system. In 1861 the 13th was given the title the Shekhawati Battalion, which became the 13th (Shekhawati Regiment) Bengal Native Infantry.

Newspapers at Launceston in Tasmania of 3 March 1858 carried the following notice:

> Killed at Cawnpore by the mutineers, Lieutenant Burnett Ashburner, Bengal Artillery, sixth son of William Page Ashburner, esq, formerly of Bombay, and grandson of the Dowager Lady Forbes.
>
> On his way to Ferozepore he halted at Allahabad, where he volunteered his services as an Artillery officer for Cawnpore, where he fell gallantly. A very promising intelligent young officer, and a great loss to his family and the Service.

Emma Larkins entrusted her letter to the Ayah known as nun-nah, who managed to get past the enemy lines and escape. When nun-nah arrived at the address in Calcutta, the man the letter was meant for would not see her, and gave no credence to her story. However, the woman broke down in tears, drew forth the packet and gave it to a servant. She raised her hands and called up to Heaven to witness that she had been faithful to the trust her mistress had placed in her, and with that she turned and walked away, never to be seen or heard of again.

The letter only got back to the family a year and nine months after it was written. Alice Larkins became Alice Pelly, who allowed the 'intensely pathetic letter' to be published in numerous newspapers throughout the Empire, under the title 'Mother's Farewell. Last Letter Out of Cawnpore"

Orphaned at the age of twelve, Charlotte Jacobi was the sole survivor of her entire family. She was still in her teens when she married James Hogan at Fort William on 13 July 1863. According to the family, they are said to have had 'a wonderful marriage' that produced thirteen children. They apparently built up a large and prosperous business, with chemist shops in Rawalpindi, Peshawar and Murree, and a transport company.

Charles Thomas Probett married Annie (formerly Shields) of Belfast on 4 November 1873. They had both been orphaned by the rebellion. Charles is believed to have become an engine driver with the East India Railway. He died on 5 January 1918 and was buried in Allahabad. Another descendant was Edwin Ernest Probett, who was born in Allahabad on 5 January 1919. Edwin is the father of Mark Probett; who has given great assistance to me throughout this project.

An eighteen-carat gold and enamel mourning ring was produced for Captain Athill Turner, which is Hallmarked 'Birmingham 1857'. It is engraved with the words 'Killed in the Massacre at Cawnpore after being brought back severely wounded from the boats. Captain Athill Turner, 1st Bengal Native Infantry, aged 37. Also died of fever in the entrenchment, Ellen, his wife, youngest daughter of the late Rev. B Pain, of Aspley Guise, Bedfordshire. NB: Their infant daughter is supposed to have died around the same time.'

There is a piscina memorial tablet in Liston Church, Essex, that states 'In memory of Robert Bensley Thornhill and Mary White, his wife, who, after 66 days and nights of extreme sufferings were, with their children, Charles Cuthbert and Mary Catherine, and their faithful nurse, Mary Long, cruelly massacred on the 15th of July 1857.'

Susan Blair's father, General Kennedy, died at Benares in 1859, and when the Prince of Wales visited there in 1876 he asked to see Mrs Kennedy. He congratulated her on her venerable age, and on the respect and affection she enjoyed. Charles Renny Blair became a lieutenant-colonel in the Indian Army and died in 1912.

There is a memorial to Captain Blair in St Michael's and St Paul's Cathedral in Bath, which includes the words 'Sacred also to the memory of Susan, wife of Captain Edward McLeod Blair, aged 49 years, and their daughters, Isabella, aged 24, and Susan aged 17, who all died at Cawnpore in June 1857.'

There is also a memorial at St Matthew's Church at Widcombe in Bath to all the family of General James Kennedy who were killed at Cawnpore.

On 24 November 1857 a letter written by Lieutenant de la Fosse appeared in the *London Gazette* recording the fates of those of whom he was certain, which confirmed the slaughter of Lieutenant Wren in the water at Sati Chaura Ghat on 27 June 1857. The application for his campaign medal was made by his eldest brother, Adderly Barton Wren, JP, in 1886. It was sanctioned in military despatch to India Number 181 of 15 July 1886, which stated:

> The late Francis Stoneham Montagu Wren, 2nd Bengal Light Cavalry, is stated on page 260 of the Bengal Army List for January 1858 to have been killed by insurgents at Cawnpore on 27th June 1857. A Mutiny medal roll of his name should therefore have been furnished by your Government, but none appears to have been received in this office. The fact of the deceased officer's being entitled to the Mutiny medal has just been brought to the notice of the next of kin, his eldest brother Mr Adderly B Wren, who has accordingly preferred an application for it. As the claim is a just one, I have sanctioned the issue of a medal, and I request that your Excellency will cause a formal medal roll to be transmitted to this office for filing with the other records.

A medal roll was duly returned with the military despatch from India of 25 October 1886, and Adderly Wren received his brother's medal on 13

December of that year. We are fortunate that the persistence of his next-of-kin resulted in the issue of a medal to commemorate the services of his brother for, in the great majority of cases, medals were not forthcoming for the families of the many officers and men massacred at Cawnpore.

A memorial tablet to the mother of Lieutenant Francis Stoneham Montagu Wren at St Margaret's Church in Northam, Devon states:

> To the memory of Delitia Montagu, wife of Major Thomas Wren of Lenwood House, youngest daughter of Admiral Barton of Burrough. Died 17 June 1836, aged 42. Also of Henry Conway, son of the above, died 12 August 1838, aged 15. Also of Francis Stoneham Montagu, their youngest son, Lieutenant in the 2nd Regiment of Bengal Cavalry who fell at Cawnpore during the Indian Mutiny in June 1857, aged 21.

The Wray Memorials in the Lady Chapel at St Andrew's Church at Aysgarth, Wensleydale, which was furnished by the Wray family, include one to 'Ann Fawcett – The Heroine of Cawnpore'.

Although listed as missing, Lieutenant Fraser actually survived the rebellion and rose to the rank of general. He married twice more and had nine children, not all of whom survived into adulthood. He died in Cheltenham on 24 May 1898, aged seventy-one.

Isabel White's brother, Henry, and sisters, Helen and Emily, placed a memorial inscription dedicated to her on their parents' gravestone at Taunton Cemetery.

A memorial tablet to Doctor Maltby and his wife was placed at St Mary's Parish Church in Shelton that reads 'Samuel Maltby, Surgeon HEICS, and Anne, his wife, only child of Lt-General G W A Lloyd CB, both massacred in the Indian Mutiny 1857. The tablet was erected by his sorrowing parents.'

A memorial tablet erected at St Peter in Thanet Church reads

> In memory of Frederick Redman Esq, Lieutenant late 1st Bengal Native Infantry, killed in action at Cawnpore between the 6th and

24th June 1857, repelling one of the assaults by mutineers and rebels on the entrenched position under Sir Hugh Wheeler. Fourth and youngest son of the late George Clavering Redman of Claringbold House, St Peter's. Aged 26.

This tablet was erected by a sorrowing brother as a tribute of affection and record of esteem, for the amiable and high character of one from whose career thus abruptly closed, so much had been fondly anticipated. 'Thy Will Be Done'.

A death notice to Lieutenant Redman in *The Times* for 27 March 1858 ended with '… and beloved brother of John Baldy Redman of 5 Terrace, New Palace Yard, Westminster. J B Redman (1816–1899) was a highly-respected designer who became a member of the Institution of Civil Engineers in 1839, and exhibited a model of the Royal Terrace Pier at Milton-on-Thames to the Great Exhibition in 1851.'

The north-west chapel of the church of St Andrew and St Mary at Pitminster has several memorials dedicated to the Vibart family, and the west wing at St Andrews Church at Old Cleeve in Somerset bears a memorial to William Leonard Halliday, his wife, Emma, and daughter, Edith, and to Edward Vibart, and his wife and four children, all of whom died at Cawnpore.

An article published in the *Illustrated London News* of 28 November 1857, stated 'The heroes of this wonderful siege were Ashe (Artillery); Moore, 32nd, and Halliday; they were amongst England's most glorious sons, and their names should ever be remembered by all who respect great deeds.'

Henrietta Louisa Vibart lived at Chapel Cleeve with her uncle, John Halliday JP and DL, and his wife, Georgina. On John's death, Henrietta and Georgina went to live at Minehead, where Henrietta died in 1926.

During restoration work in the 1950s a stained–glass lancet memorial window was discovered at St James the Great Church in Thorley dedicated to Lieutenant Bax.

Captain Hayes, Lieutenant Barbour and Richard Fayrer were buried at St Paul's Churchyard in Mainpuri. The inscription on the tomb of Captain

Hayes, which was erected by his bereaved mother, reads 'He was an accomplished scholar and a distinguished soldier.' He was also described as 'an Oriental scholar of distinction, an able and skilful diplomatist, a man of great ability, area courage and unbounded ambition.'

Richard Fayrer's oldest brother was Joseph Fayrer MD, a prominent surgeon of the Bengal Army stationed at Lucknow, who placed a tombstone at the church that reads 'In affectionate remembrance of his brother.'

There is a white scroll memorial dedicated to Captain Robert Urquhart Jenkins at St John's Church at Beachey in the Forest of Dean, Gloucestershire, which says 'Died at Cawnpore 1857, 3 Days before the surrender to the infamous Nana Sahib.'

A brass memorial plaque dedicated to Melville Balfour was placed in the original chapel at Radley College, and was moved to its present place in the new chapel in 1895. Its translation reads 'In pious memory of Melville Balfour, a former pupil, who was massacred at Cawnpore, 1857. Jesus have mercy.'

There is a memorial to Lieutenant Sotheby of the Bengal Artillery at St John the Evangelist Church in Clifton near Preston, and at St John's Church in Lytham. His mother died at Salwick Hall near Preston on 18 December 1862, and at the time of his death in 1886 his stepfather was compiling *A History of the Old County Regiment of Lancashire Militia*, which was published in 1888.

Ensigns John Wright Henderson and Ensign Robert William Henderson were the two eldest sons of the Reverend Robert Henderson MA, who was the incumbent of the Holy Trinity Episcopal Church in Stirling for forty years. They are commemorated on their father's gravestone at the Old Town Cemetery in Stirling.

A memorial at Balmoral Cemetery in Malone, Belfast, reads 'In memory of Alexander Moncrieff, 19th February 1864, aged 68 years. Also of his son, the Rev. E T R Moncrieff LLD, Chaplain to the H E I Co's service, who, with his wife and child, were murdered at Cawnpore during the Mutiny, June 1857.'

Lieutenant Swynfen Jervis's brother, William, took part in the capture of Delhi and the relief of Lucknow; during which time his regiment gained five Victoria Crosses. He became a first-class cricketer. He played in a first class match for the Gentlemen of Kent in 1865, taking six wickets for 30 runs in the second innings, and while his regiment was stationed at Bury in Lancashire he played for the Western Club at Monton in Eccles, the Broughton Cricket Club in Salford, and the Manchester Cricket Club, and during this time he was selected to play four matches for Cheshire CCC in 1873, and in the first class match at Old Trafford on 6 and 7 June 1874 between Lancashire and Derbyshire.

A silent movie historical drama entitled *The Beggar of Cawnpore* was produced in 1916, under the direction of Charles Swickard. It was set against the backdrop of the Indian Rebellion.

Chetham's Library in Manchester hold an advertisement presenting one of Belle Vue's world famous fireworks displays that depicted well known historical events. One is entitled 'India: The Massacre of Cawnpore' – and is described as 'A stupendous, breath-taking spectacle'

In 2012 Tom Williams produced a historical novel of fiction entitled *Cawnpore (The Williamson Papers, book 2)*, which features the Hillersdon family.

The 32nd Light Infantry famously defended Lucknow from July to November 1857, and the regiment's brigadier was in overall command of the troops in the Lucknow garrison during the siege. The regiment was renamed the 32nd (Cornwall) Light Infantry in recognition of its contribution during the rebellion. All four Victoria Crosses gained by the unit were for gallantry at Lucknow, and are now in their rightful place at the Duke of Cornwall's Regimental Museum at The Keep in Bodmin, Cornwall. A memorial dedicated to and detailing the losses suffered by the 32nd Light Infantry is located at the Devonshire Regimental Chapel inside the west entrance to Exeter Cathedral.

Medals to men of the 32nd who were murdered at Cawnpore are very rare and it is probable that for the most part they remained unclaimed and were eventually returned to be melted down. Some twelve examples are known to have survived. Some 32nd Regiment Indian Mutiny medals awarded to victims of the massacres have been offered at auctions. In 2005, those of Captain Moore, Colour-Sergeant John Johnson (the senior NCO of the regiment at Cawnpore); and Private John Overmass; in 2009 Private G. W. Johnson; and in 2015 Sergeant Magwood.

Private Bannister's Indian Mutiny Medal was traced to a private collection, and was sold at auction in 2015. His earlier Sutlej, Punjab and India General Service Medals were almost certainly lost at Cawnpore. The owner of his one surviving medal was Vivian Stuart, a military novelist who had used Bannister as one of her characters in her 2003 novel *Massacre at Cawnpore*.

Private Bannister's great nephew came upon his 'India Letters' in 1974; these included the last-known reference to John's fate, dated March 1860, stating that he had no effects and the matter of any prize money due should be taken up with the authorities at the Royal Chelsea Hospital. The family loaned the letters to the National Army Museum, and copies are held in the museum's archive.

As part of the Childers Reforms of 1881 the regiment was merged with the 46th (South Devonshire) Regiment to form the Duke of Cornwall's Light Infantry. As part of the 1957 Defence White Paper in 1959 it merged with the Somerset Light Infantry (Prince Albert's) to form the Somerset and Cornwall Light Infantry. It then merged with several other Light Infantry units in 2004 to form the Light Infantry, which in 2007 merged with three other regiments as part of the Future Army Structure to form The Rifles, which carries on the lineage of the 32nd, and has seen active service in Iraq and Afghanistan, gaining many gallantry awards.

The 84th (York and Lancaster) Regiment also famously defended the Lucknow Residency. It gained no fewer than six Victoria Crosses for gallantry in and around the city, of which four are held at the York and Lancaster Museum at Clifton Park in Rotherham, South Yorkshire.

The 84th was saluted from the battery of Fort William upon leaving Calcutta in 1859 (one of only two regiments to be so honoured) after seventeen years in India. On return to England they were stationed in Sheffield, where they received an address of welcome from the mayor, and the men were presented with penknives from the Cutlers' Company. Private Murphy was asked by senior officers of the regiment to record an account of the siege of Cawnpore.

Medals to men of the unit who died at Cawnpore have occasionally been sold at auction. These include sales in 2005 the Turkish Crimea Medal and Indian Mutiny Medal of Lieutenant Saunders; and in 2011 the campaign medal of Private Mallinson.

As part of the Childers reforms of 1881, the 84th merged with the 65th (2nd Yorkshire, North Riding) Regiment to become the York and Lancaster Regiment. In 1968 the unit became the only English regiment to choose to disband rather than form an amalgamation with another regiment.

The 1st Madras (European) Fusiliers gained four Victoria Crosses for the campaign. It was taken into the British Army in 1858 as the 1st Madras Fusiliers, adding the word 'Royal' in 1861, and in the following year it was named the 102nd Regiment of Foot (Royal Madras Fusiliers). In 1881 it merged with the 103rd (Bombay) Regiment of Foot to become the 1st Battalion, Royal Dublin Fusiliers. The regiment was disbanded at the formation of the Irish Free State (Republic of Ireland) in 1922.

The Bengal Artillery gained seventeen Victoria Crosses for operations at various engagements during the Indian Rebellion, such as Delhi, Lucknow, Bulandshahr, and the operations in central India under Sir Hugh Rose. The most notable of these was the five gained for valour during the bombardment of the Shah Najaf, performed as the troops under Sir Colin Campbell fought their way to the second relief of the Lucknow Residency, on 16–17 November 1857. They were some of the twenty-four that were gained during the two days of fighting – the most Victoria Crosses gained within a single twenty-four-hour period in the history of the medal. After 1860 the East India Company's units were absorbed into the Royal Regiment of Artillery.

At that time the Victoria Cross was not awarded to men who did not live to wear it, and had the rules been different it is certain that several would have been received by the defenders of the Cawnpore Garrison.

In addition to this, had there been an equivalent civilian medal available at the time, such as the George Cross or the George Medal, a number of the defenders would also have received such a medal for their gallantry – including women.

Mowbray Thomson spoke of two men, who acted as cooks, who braved the gauntlet of fierce enemy fire to bring the meagre but welcome ration of food to the outer barracks where he was stationed:

> If ever men deserved the Victoria Cross these poor fellows did; nor were they the only ones of our garrison who in all probability would have earned this distinction, so dear to the soldiers of modern times. But as the heroes before Agamemnon lost their need of applause for want of a poet, so some in later times, through the loss of superior officers, and having none left to report upon their deeds, have only reserved to them the consciousness of having done all that human endurance could accomplish to sustain the honour of the British arms.

He also recorded the 'rare heroism' of Ann Fawcett Fraser:

> During the horrors of the siege she won the admiration of all our party by her indefatigable attentions to the wounded. Neither danger nor fatigue seemed to have power to suspend her ministry of mercy.

Based on the citations for the actions during the campaign for which gallantry medals were awarded, and my knowledge attained over four decades of studying the criteria for such awards, I believe that the following individuals would have been considered. The list is by no means exhaustive, and I believe the total number would have risen to double figures. However, only Lieutenant de la Fosse would have actually received an award because he is the only one who survived, but none of the senior officers who witnessed his bravery survived to make an official report.

Captain John Moore, 32nd (Cornwall) Light Infantry. This officer showed great leadership, fine example and excellent behaviour under the most trying circumstances. He was involved in a number of daring actions and gave solace and encouragement to others while under fire.

Lieutenant Frederick John Gothleipe Saunders, 84th (York and Lancaster) Regiment. For his gallant action in attempting to assassinate the leader of the rebels knowing he had no chance of escape and that he would, and did, suffer dreadful consequences.

Lieutenant St George Ashe, Bengal Artillery. For directing the fire of the guns in his battery with great accuracy and effect, while showing a complete disregard for his own safety which undoubtedly inspired the men around him.

Lieutenant Henry George de la Fosse, 53rd Bengal Native Infantry. For risking his life to extinguish a fire which, had it not been dealt with by him, would have ignited ammunition in the battery and therefore his action almost certainly saved many lives.

Two anonymous men, who risked their lives to provide food for their comrades in the outposts within the barracks, and several others who also braved the perilous danger to provide ammunition to the same.

Ann Fawcett Fraser (civilian). She showed complete disregard for her own well-being as she offered assistance and encouragement to those around her even though she herself was suffering from injury and fatigue so severe that her constitution eventually broke down.

I also note here that the gallant actions of John Bensley Thornhill were at least equal to those of Henry Kavanagh, who was awarded a rare civilian Victoria Cross for leaving the Residency and leading Colin Campbell's column through Lucknow for the second relief in the following November. John was also one of the Lucknow garrison, and on the approach of Havelock's relieving force in September, he volunteered to go out and guide the troops through the city, being mortally wounded in this gallant service. It is likely that he too would have received the Victoria Cross had he survived.

Victims of the Bibighar

A number of notes were found among the carnage. One of them was written by Caroline Lindsay that stated:

Entered the barracks May 21st
Cavalry left June 5th
First shot fired June 6th
Aunt Lily died June 17th
Uncle Willy died June 18th
Left barracks June 27th
Made prisoners as soon as we were at the river
George died June 27th
Alice died July 9th
Mamma died July 12th

Colonel Ramsey was of the opinion that the note also stated:

> 'On such a date we surrendered ourselves. Got into boats when we were fired upon. Those of us who escaped taken prisoner and brought into this room, where …'

Here the journal ends abruptly.

In a Bible belonging to the Blair family, who escaped in Vibart's boat and were later recaptured, it was written:

27th June. Went to the boats
29th. Taken out of boats
30th. Taken to Savada Kothi. Fatal day

Various newspapers of 19 October 1857 carried the following report:

The Cawnpore Massacre

Two hundred and thirty women and children, says an eyewitness to the horrors perpetrated at this station, were put to death in the most cruel manner by the mutineers; the whole of their clothing was torn to pieces and their bodies left in a state of nudity; even the hair of their head was pulled out by the roots, the heads and bodies were mangled and hacked to pieces; they rest, says he, in a large well in the compound.

It is stated by Captain Herbert Bruce, Superintendent of Police at Cawnpore, that almost all the former European residents there were murdered by the miscreant Nana Sing; the only Europeans who escaped being two officers and two soldiers who fled across the river, and one pensioner of the 3rd Light Dragoons, who was concealed by a trooper of the 4th Light Cavalry in the city of Cawnpore.

From another source, we learn that a note was found written in Hindu, containing the names of all the ladies who died between the 7th and 15th July, from what are described as natural causes. The list appears to have been kept by a native doctor, and deducting the names which it contains it appears that 197 persons were massacred on the evening of the 15th. The names were not easy to make out, but they are something like the following:

7th (July) – 3 persons died (names not given); Mrs. Keelan, cholera; Mrs Boyce, dysentery.

8th – Miss Glasgow, cholera; Mrs Heles (name indistinct), wounds; Mrs Harlow, cholera; Colonel Wieger's little boy, diarrhoea.

10th – Miss Lindsay (probably on the previous day): Miss Fedharnn (Fraser?), cholera; Mrs Liundel's boy, cholera; Mrs Charley (Greenway), cholera. According to Andrew Ward, Louisa Chalwin died of disease in this day.

11th – Mrs Reid's child, diarrhoea.

12th – Dr Muir's girl (name doubtful), diarrhoea; Mrs Lindsay, wound in the back; Marianne Conolly, cholera; William Simpson, cholera.

13th – Mrs Greenway's supposed to be ayah, diarrhoea; Mrs Bristow, diarrhoea; Mr Brett's girl, diarrhoea.

14th – Mr Greenway, diarrhoea; James Lee, diarrhoea.

16th (probably 15th) – Thomas Barker and Mrs Gurney, diseases not named.

The building in which the massacre took place is described as looking like a slaughter house.

The Victims

It is unlikely that there will ever be an accurate roll of all the victims who were massacred in the Bibighar. However, the following list is based on the information from the JWB Historical Library. Note: (F) means that they arrived at Cawnpore from the Fatehgarh garrison)

Mrs Baines (or Bayne, possibly the wife of J. C. Bayne, a railway engineer)
Phillip Baines
Mrs Battie
Mrs Barking
Mrs Bell
Alpen Bell
Eliza Bennett
Ellen Margaret Fitzgerald Berrill
Catherine Berrill
Mrs Berthwick
Mrs Susan Blair
Susan Blair

Mrs Breck (or Brett)
Henry Brett
Miss C Burn
Miss Burn
(This is probably Mary Burne and 1 child of the 32nd Regiment)

George Caley
C. Caley
Mrs Carroll
Miss Carroll
(This is probably Mary Carroll and 1 child of the 32nd Regiment)
Mrs Carter
Mary Cheeters (Mrs Prout's maidservant)
Mrs Colgan
Mrs Cook
Mrs Cooper
(F) Mrs Copeland
Mrs Copeman
Maria Conway
Miss Conway
James Cousins
Miss Crabb

Mrs Dallas
Mrs Daly
Mrs Mary Anne Darby (and infant)
Jane Birrell Dempster (Mrs D. on list)
Charles Dempster
Henry Dempster
William Dempster
Henry Duncan
Weston Dundi (or Dundas)
Mrs Dupton
Charles Dupton
William Dupton
Henry Dupton

(possibly Dutton – Joseph Dutton married Seraphina 'Fanny' Gamboa at Cawnpore on 6 May 1814. Their daughter, Frances 'Fanny' Elizabeth Dutton, was born on 11 March 1819. She married Evan Forsyth at Allahabad on 2 September 1833, and died in the Cawnpore massacre with three of her children, her sister, and the children of her sister).

Margaret Fitzgerald
Mary Fitzgerald
Tom Fitzgerald
Ellen Fitzgerald
John Fitzgerald

J. Gill (child)
Mrs Gillie
(F) Mrs Gillom
Mrs Gilpin
Harriet Gilpin
Sarah Gilpin
Sam Gilpin
S. Gilpin
(F) Mrs Goldie
(F) Mary Goldie
(F) Eliza Goldie
Mrs Green
Edward Green
Mrs Rose Anne Greenway?
Jane Greenway
Mary Greenway
Margaret Greenway
Martha Greenway
John Greenway
Y. Greenway
Mrs Eliza Guthrie
Catherine Guthrie

(F) Gertrude Lowther Sandham Heathcote
(F) Godfrey Heathcote
(The monument at Fatehgarh states two children)
Mrs Hill
Elizabeth 'Lizzie' Holmes

Mrs (Henry) Jacobi
Henry Jacobi, junior
Hugh Jacobi
Lucy Jacobi
William James
Mrs (Arthur) Jenkins
Mrs A. R. Johnson
Mrs Jones

Grace Kirk
William Kirk
Charlotte Kirk
Mrs Kurside
Henry Kurside
Willis Kurside

Nancy Lang
Mrs Lery
James Lery
C. Lery
James Lewis
Caroline Lindsay
Frances 'Fanny' Lindsay
(F) Godfrey Lloyd
(F) Bela Lloyd
(F)Miss Mary Long
(F) Mrs Emma McCausland Lowis
(F) Emma Maria Lowis
(F) Eliza Lowis
(F) Mrs Lupin
Lucy Lyell

Mrs MacCuller
Mrs Mackinna
(F) Mrs Anne Maltby
Jervie Martindale
Mrs Caroline Edith Moore
? Moore
Mrs Jane Morfett
Mrs Murray

Charlotte Newenham (sister of Susan Blair)
Mrs Norris
William North

Mrs J. L. O'Brien
Miss O'Connor

Mrs Parrott
Mrs Peel
George Peel
Mrs Peters
Miss Peters
James Peters
Mary Peters
Harriet Pistol
Mrs Pokeson
Mrs Ellen Walsh Probett
Amy Ruth Probett
Emma Probett
Louise Probett
Nellie Probett
Johnnie Probett
William Stephen Probett
Mrs Prout

Mrs Raselier
(F) Mrs Reen

(F) Mary Reen
(F) Catherine Reen
(F) Eliza Reen
(F) Lucy Reen
(F) Jane Reen
(F) Dina Reen
(F) Emalia Reen
(F) Mrs Rees
(F) Eliza Rees
(F) Jane Rees
Mrs Reid
James Reid
Julia Reid
C. Reid
Charles Reid
Baby Reid
Mrs Roach
Mrs Russell
Eliza Russell

Eliza Sanpore
Mrs Sarah Saunders
Frederick Herbert Saunders
Mrs Scott
Jessie Seppings
John James Seppings
Edward Matthew Seppings
Mrs Seth (or Setts)
Mrs N. Sheridan
William Sheridan
Baby Sheridan
Henry Simpson
Miss Sinclair
(F) Mrs Mary Smith
(F) Child Smith
Lucy Stake

William Stake
(The monument at Fatehgarh mentions a Mrs Sturt and two children)

(F) Mrs Thompson
(F) Mary White Siddons Thornhill
(F) Charles Cudbert Thornhill
(F) Mary Catherine Thornhill
Mrs Tibbetts
(F) Mrs Louisa Isabella Tucker
(F) Annie Tucker
(F) Louisa Tucker
(F) George Tucker
(F) L. Tucker
(F) Miss Tucker
Mrs Twoomy and child

Mrs Walker
Daniel Walker
Mrs Wallet
(F) Mrs West
Elizabeth West
Emma Weston
George Weston
Mrs White
(32nd – Mary White and 1 child)
Isabella Georgina White
Bridget Widdowson
Catherine Widlep
Jane Widlep
Thomas Widlep
Henry Williams
Miss Williams
Mrs Mary Blanchard Bray Williams
Georgina Williams
Frances 'Fanny' Williams
Mrs Willis

Mrs Wooller
Tommy Wooller
Susan Wooller
(F) Mrs Woolcar
(F) Charles Woolcar
(F) Thomas Woolcar
Mrs Wrixam
Clara Lucy Wrixam
Edward (Drummond) Wrixam

Mrs Yates (Yatman)

Two Ayahs
(F) Three Ayahs

The Cawnpore Massacres by
Mowbray Thomson

In response to a statement made in the *Indian Empire* on 3 September 1858, by Mrs Murray, the wife of Sergeant-Major Murray, Captain Mowbray Thomson had the following article published in *The Times* on 8 September 1858:

The Cawnpore Massacre

Sir – Justice to the dead compels me to beg of you to give place in your valuable journal to my emphatic contradiction of the account of the Cawnpore massacre transferred to your columns on the 3d inst. From those of the *Indian Empire*, and alleged to be the statement of Mrs Murray, the wife of Sergeant-Major Murray. It is not for me to conjecture by what means this poor woman has been induced to give utterance to such a version of our troubles at Cawnpore as she has done, but I feel bound to correct her narrative, and I feel sure that my brother officer, Lieutenant Delafosse, who is in this country, will be able to substantiate the allegations I now make.

After a truthful reference to the general uneasiness pervading the native mind which preceded the outbreak, Mrs Murray states that General Wheeler ordered a parade, and read a general order discontinuing the old musket, and directing the use of the Enfield rifle for the future. She says: 'The Sepoys refused to use the new guns. Parade was again ordered with no better results.' Now, sir, I affirm that there was not an Enfield rifle in Cawnpore until 15 men of the 1st Madras Fusiliers joined us two days before the outbreak, and these were the only men in Cawnpore armed with that weapon. I have no knowledge of the imprisonment of General Wheeler of the havildar who reported the disaffection of the native troops. I believe it is as untrue as the foregoing story of the Enfield rifles.

Nana Sahib's visit to Cawnpore, which is next referred to, was made at the request of the resident magistrate, and such was the confidence placed in this infernal traitor that the whole of the treasure – upwards of 100,000*l* was placed under his protection. The Nana was not at Bithoor, but in Cawnpore – when the 2nd Cavalry mutinied and he gave up the treasure to the rebels. This was the first manifestation of hostility on his part. A day or two before it was actually projected to send some of our ladies to Bithoor, that they might be lodged in safety! All the European residents of Cawnpore, except the officers of the 53rd Native Infantry, were in the entrenched buildings several days before the actual outburst. Here, again, Mrs Murray is made to represent the facts erroneously. It is some nameless correspondent of the *Indian Empire* – or Mrs Murray – whose knowledge of artillery is so profound as to lead to the conclusion that shells did not harm because they were *only filled with powder?* These shells cut off numbers of our poor comrades, though Mrs Murray is made to say that very few were killed in the entrenchments, and only one or two by shells. So far is this from being the case that we lost 250 men in the entrenchment in 22 days, and a large number of these were killed by shells; certainly as many as a dozen on one fatal day that I remember.

Not one of our killed was sewn in a bag (as it is stated) previously to internment; we had neither materials nor time for such labour. At nightfall each day the slain were buried as decently as circumstances would permit. Alas! It was little more we could do than place them under ground.

The statement that little children were sent to draw water is an invention; this task was always performed by volunteers, and some of our privates of the European regiments made a trade of it, charging so much per bucket.

The sally said to have been contrived by consultation among the troops was an orderly assault upon the batteries of the besiegers, headed by Captain Moore, 32nd Foot, with the full consent of General Wheeler. No retreat was sounded, and they returned in due order when their work was done, and not before. It was as cool a thing as was ever seen in war, deserving of very different comment from that in the *Indian Empire*. 'Not more than 30 soldiers were killed in the garrison.' Says Mrs Murray. The whole of the artillerymen at the station, 59 in number, were killed at their guns, except four or five, who survived till the embarkation. Our force of European troops at the time of the outbreak consisted of 59 artillerymen, 75 of the 32nd Regiment (invalids), 15 of the 1st Madres Fusiliers, and about 50 of the 84th Foot, about 200 in all. I am sure that 100 of these fell during the siege.

Mrs Murray is represented as saying, that to the best of her knowledge there were lots of provisions in the garrison, and insinuates that General Wheeler might have held out a fortnight longer. Yet I know that two persons died of starvation, a horse was greedily devoured, and some of my men were glad to feed upon a dog. Our daily supply of provisions for 22 days consisted of half-a-pint of pea soup and two or three chuppaties (or cakes made of flour) these last being together about the size of an Abernethy biscuit. Upon this diet, which was served to all without distinction – officers and privates, civilians or soldiers – the garrison was reduced to a company of spectres long before the period of capitulation, and when this took place there were only four days' rations, at the above rate of supply, in stock.

I do not believe that General Wheeler manifested the slightest desire to capitulate. I know that he opposed it heartily, and only succumbed upon the strong representations of the second in command, an officer exemplary for his courage – the very life sinews of our beleaguered band, but wholly inexperienced in native character. The younger officers were at the time advocates for resistance to the last; but, looking back calmly upon all the perils of those never-to-be-forgotten days, and considering that which I am sure mainly influenced the decision – viz, the horrible exposure of multitudes of women and children – I much doubt whether the slightest censure should rest upon either of my senior officers for the steps taken. They were all brave men, and I should be most unworthy of the preservations so wonderfully extended to me if I did not retrieve their memory from undeserved reproach. During the whole period of our straits in the entrenchment there was not one instance of dejection through cowardice. The very children seemed inspired with heroic patience, and our women behaved with a fortitude that only English women could have shown.

There are other statements equally erroneous in this most injurious publication, which, comparatively harmless in the pages of the *Indian Empire*, has acquired world-wide celebrity by transfer to *The Times*. I cannot prolong my refutation, lest it should be excluded from your columns. I hope ere long, in an account of my escapes and experiences at Cawnpore, to be able to set at rest all doubts that may have been raised touching the honour of my much-lamented companions, and to assure survivors in England that their grief need not be embittered by the suspicion of incompetency or ill conduct on the part of any engaged in a scene that will not soon cease to be talked and thought of in our fatherland.

Appendix III

Haileybury

Several people involved in the incidents around Cawnpore were educated at Haileybury College in Hertfordshire, which was a school for children of East India Company employees and prepared its students for service with their father's company. In 1894 the college published: *Memorials of Old Haileybury College: Former Pupils of the Honourable East India College 'Old Haileybury' Who Died in the Service of their Country*. The following are edited extracts from that publication:

Robert Tudor Tucker
1833–1835

To the south of Cawnpore, Robert Tucker was the judge of Futtehpore. On June 9 the storm burst at this Station. The mob plundered the Treasury, let loose the prisoners and destroyed the Government offices, and the officials had to escape as best they could. But Tucker refused to stir. He took up his post on the roof of the Magistrate's office and there held the rebels at bay till he was shot down, not before several had fallen to his rifle. Not one member of the Service behaved more gallantly than Robert Tucker, one brave Englishman alone and unsupported, not hesitating to face an infuriated mob of ruffians and sacrificing the life which he might well have saved to a noble, if exaggerated, sense of duty. So much had he endeared himself to all that after his death two Hindus stood out and cursed his murderers in public, for which honest and brave speech they lost their lives.

(Robert was a son of Henry St George Tucker of Edinburgh, who was chairman and a director of the East India Company)

Robert Bensley Thornhill
1835–1837

Judge of Farruckabad, a station eighty miles up the Ganges from
Cawnpore. It was garrisoned by the 10th Native Infantry, which did
not commit any overt act of mutiny till 3 June, when some of the Oudh
Irregulars entered the station and the 10th fraternized with them. A few
days later the 41st Native Infantry, which had mutinied and committed
many murders at Seetapore, arrived and the city rose, thus rendering the
place untenable. Some of the residents had previously gone down the
river in boats, the rest took the fort, which they gallantly defended to the
last. Thornhill was one of the fugitives in the boats, many of whom were
killed on the voyage. The rest only reached Bithoor to swell the terrible
slaughter carried out there and at Cawnpore by the orders of the Nana.

(Robert had two brothers educated at Haileybury who were involved in
incidents in Oudh during the uprising, and they both lost their lives.)

Charles George Hillersdon
1838–1840

Collector of Cawnpore. This is not the place to record the events of the
terribly anxious times passed by the Christians of Cawnpore previous
to entering the so-called entrenchment, nowhere higher than three feet,
which they did as a forlorn hope; nor the terrible suffering they there
underwent; nor the cruel treachery of which the survivors were victims,
trusting to the promised protection and safeguard of the accursed Nana.
Suffice it to say the brave and patient Hillersdon soon fell, killed by a
round shot in the presence of his wife, she herself soon following him.

Captain Edward Charles Vibart
1842

2nd Bengal Light Cavalry; killed at Cawnpore on 27 June 1857.

Henry Bensley Thornhill
1844–1845

Assistant Commissioner of Seetapore in Oudh. This station was garrisoned by the 41st Native Infantry, a regiment which gained an unenviable notoriety in the Mutiny. The residents held out as long as possible, but had to leave after terrible anxieties. They were hotly pursued, and men women and children ruthlessly shot down by the mutineers. Thornhill and his wife perished amongst them.

John Robert Mackillop
1844–1846

Joint Magistrate of Cawnpore; a brave, unselfish man. When the English entered what was called the entrenchment, which were hastily thrown up earthworks, affording little or no shelter to the besieged, Mackillop took upon himself to draw water for his comrades from a well exposed to the full fire of the rebels. He did not long carry on this dangerous duty, but soon fell a victim to his unselfish bravery, pierced by the bullets of the enemy. No man ever yielded his life better than 'Jack' Mackillop.

Robert Nesbitt Lowis
1849–1851

Joint Magistrate of Farruckabad, close to the cantonment of Futtehgurh. On hearing of the approach of the mutineers from Bareilly and Shahjehanpore, the non-combatants set off in boats down the Ganges. But hearing many contradictory reports as to the attitude of the villagers on the banks, the party divided next day. Some went up the Ramganga to Dharmpore, whence most of them returned to Futtehgurh. This they gallantly defended, but were eventually obliged to evacuate it and the survivors were brutally murdered. The others tried to escape down the Ganges to Cawnpore and Lowis went with them. He lost his life on the way; the others were victims of the Nana at Bithoor.

John Bensley Thornhill
1850–1852

Deputy Commissioner in Oudh. Was one of the Lucknow garrison, having escaped from his own district. On the approach of Havelock's relieving force Thornhill volunteered to go out and guide the troops through the city. In the performance of this most important service he was mortally wounded and died after he had been carried to the Residency.

Arthur Jenkins
1850–1852

Assistant-Commissioner at Poorwa in Oudh. Escorted the non-combatants to Cawnpore, and perished there with the rest.

(In fact, he escorted them to Aurangabad not Cawnpore. A letter from Mr Jenkins informed Mr Thomason (at Muhamdi) that the troops at Shahjahanpur had mutinied, that he and a body of fugitives, amongst whom were women and children, had reached Powain, that the Rajah of that place had refused them shelter, and it begged that all the available carriage might be sent out to bring in the fugitives to Muhamdi. Mr Thomason complied with Mr Jenkins's request).

Research Sources and Further Reading

The main procedure followed for the research of the biographical tributes was firstly to consult Edward Blunt's book on the inscriptions of tombs in Oudh, which includes some basic biographical snippets, and there are a few websites that contain some added information. Then I included information taken from my own JWB Historical Library, which I compiled over the last four decades and is now I believe to be one of the largest independent libraries of its kind. The next step was to put all the information collected together and check on sites such as Ancestry.com and Forces-War-Records.co.uk, to establish if the information was correct (which in many cases proved to be inaccurate). I then contacted the archives and local studies departments in the towns and cities associated with the victims and followed up and compared what information they could provide. I then distributed the biographies to the families of descendants I have contacted and requested their view on the contents, although I still reserved the right to use my own judgement of what was fact-based on official documentation.

The BBC's *British Empire Magazine* published in 1971 has been a mine of general information about the subject. It includes issues by respected writers concerning the history of the British in India and the British Empire in general. Further reading and research material are as follows:

Adelaide Journal, the: Last Link with the Indian Mutiny: Death of the Hero of Cawnpore (With a portrait of Sir Mowbray Thomson), 1 March 1917.

Alexander, William Gordon: *Recollections of a Highland Subaltern during the Campaigns of the 93rd Highlanders in India, under Colin Campbell, Lord Clyde, in 1857, 1858 and 1859*, 1898.

Ancestry.com

Anderson, Claire: *Subaltern Lives: Biographies of Colonialism in the Indian Ocean World, 1790–1920*, 2012.

Annual Register, the: *A Review of the History and Politics of the Year 1857*, 1858.

Annual Register, the: *A Review of Public Events at Home and Abroad for the Year 1917*, 1917.

Army Lists.

Bahadur, Sir Syed Ahmed Khan: *The Causes of the Indian Revolt*, 1859.

Ball, Charles: *The History of the Indian Mutiny*, 1858.

Bamfield, Veronica: *On the Strength: The Story of the British Army Wife*, 1974.

Bancroft, James W: *The Victoria Cross Roll of Honour*, 1989.

Bancroft, James W: *Devotion to Duty*, 1990.

Bancroft, James W: *The Chronological Roll of the Victoria Cross*, unpublished.

Bannister, Private John, 32nd Regiment: *Indian Letters, 1842–1854*, National Army Museum.

Bennett, Amelia: *Ten Month's Captivity After the Massacre at Cawnpore: The Nineteenth Century and After*, Part I, June 1913; Part II, July 1913.

Berkshire Family History Society.

Bingham, Major George; 64th (2nd Staffordshire) Regiment: *His Diary, held at the National Army Museum*, 1857.

Blunt, Alison: *Embodying War: British Women and Domestic Defilement in the Indian Mutiny, 1857–58*, Journal of Historical Geography, number 26, 2000.

Blunt, Edward Arthur Henry: *List of Inscriptions on Christian Tombs and Tablets of Historical Interest in the United Provinces of Agra and Oudh*, 1911.

Breckon, Ian: *The Bloodiest Record in the Book of Time, Amy Horne and the Indian Uprising of 1857, in Fact and Fiction*, 2012.

British Empire BBC Magazines, 1971.

British Library: Asian and African Studies.

Buckland CIE, Charles Edward: *Dictionary of Indian Biography*, 1906.

Busteed, Henry Elmsley: *Echoes from Old Calcutta*, 1882.

Chalwin, Louise: Letter written to her sister Maria on 30 April 1857, held at the India Office Library.

Cheltenham Chronicle, the: 10 February 1923.

Chick, Noah Alfred (author) and Hutchinson, David (editor): *Annals of the Indian Rebellion, 1857–58*, 1974.

Colburn's United Services Gazette, Part II, 1858.

Cornwall Light Infantry Museum at Bodmin.

Courcy, Anne de: *Fishing Fleet*, 2012.

Crump, Lieutenant Charles Wade: *A Pictorial Record of the Cawnpore Massacre*, 1858.

Cumbrian Records Office: *A. F. Huddleston in India. Digest of Indian Overseas News. 'The Insurrection' – Death notices include those 'Massacred at Cawnpore', 1857*.

David, Saul: *The Indian Mutiny*, 2004.

De la Fosse, Claude Fraser: *History of India*, 1917.

Derbyshire Records Office: Wright Family of Eyam Hall, Derbyshire. Peter Wright refers to friends and relations murdered at Cawnpore, 1857.

Dictionary of Indian Biography.

Dodd, George: *The History of the Indian Revolt, and the Expeditions to Persia, China and Japan, 1856–7–8*, 1859.

Eden, Honourable Emily: Up the Country: Letters Written to Her Sister from the Upper Provinces of India, 1867.

Edwardes, Michael: *Battles of the Indian Mutiny*, 1970.

Edwardes, Michael: *The Assault on India: British Empire Magazine*, Volume One, 1971.

Edwardes, Michael: *The Coming of the Raj. British Empire Magazine*, Volume One, 1971.

Edwardes, Michael: *The India Mutiny: British Empire Magazine*, Volume Two, 1971.

Edwardes, Michael: *A Season in Hell: The Defence of the Lucknow Residency*, 1973.

Edwardes, Michael: *Red Year: The Indian Rebellion of 1857*, 1975.

English, Barbara: *The Kanpur Massacres in India and the Revolt of 1857*, 1994.

Ewart, Emma: Three letters from Cawnpore dated 15 May, 27 May and 1 June 1857, held at the India Office Library of the British Library, reference Mss Eur B 267.

FIBIS – Families in British India Society.

Findmypast.co.uk

Fitchett, Drummer John (6th Bengal Native Infantry): His Account of the Massacre at Cawnpore given to the Court of Investigation at Meerut, 1859.

Fitchett, Reverend William Henry: *The Tale of the Great Mutiny*, 1901.

Fitzgerald, Valerie: *Zemindar*, 1983.

Forrest, George W: *A History of the Indian Mutiny, 1857–58, Reviewed and Illustrated from Original Documents*, 1904.

Foxearth and District Local History Society, the.

Fuller, Martin: *The Life and Death of Private Bannister, Medal News*, March 1998.

Germon, Maria Vincent: *A Diary Kept by Mrs R. C. Germon, at Lucknow, Between the Months of May and December, 1857, 1870*

Gubbins, Martin Richard (Bengal Civil Service): An Account of the Mutinies in Oudh, and the siege of the Lucknow Residency, 1858.

Gupta, Prakash Chandra: *Nana Sahib and the Rising at Cawnpore*, 1963.

Guthrie D. D., Thomas: *His Autobiography, and a Memoir by his Sons*, 1874.

Haileybury College, Memorials of Old: Former Pupils of the Honourable East India College 'Old Haileybury' Who Died in the Service of their Country, 1894.

Harcourt, George John: *The Regimental Records of the First Battalion, The Royal Dublin Fusiliers, Formerly the Madras Europeans, the Madras European Regiment, the First Madras Fusiliers, the 102nd Royal Madras Fusiliers, 1644– 1842, by one whose whole service was passed in the Corps and who had the honour of commanding it*, 1910.

Hibbert, Christopher: *The Great Mutiny*, 1978.

Holloway, John (32nd Light Infantry): *Essays on the Indian Mutiny*, 1866.

Huddleston, George: History of the East India Railway, 1906.

Illustrated London News, various 1857.

Indian Medical Service Listings.

Indian Journal of Surgery, 2006.

Inglis, The Honourable Lady Julia Selina: *The Siege of Lucknow: A Diary*, 1892.

Jocelyn, Colonel Julian Robert John: *History of the Royal and Indian Artillery in the Mutiny of 1857*, 1915.

Kadina and Wallaroo Times, South Australia, 2 March 1895.

Kaye, Sir John: *History of the Sepoy War, 1857–58*, (Volumes 1 and 2) 1878.

Leckey, Edward: *Fictions Connected with the Indian Outbreak of 1857 Exposed*, 1859.

Lee, Joseph W: *The Indian Mutiny, and in Particular a Narrative of the Events at Cawnpore, June and July 1857*, 1884.

Lee, John Fitzgerald, and Radcliffe, Captain Frederick Walter: *The Indian Mutiny up to the Relief of Lucknow, November 17th, 1857*, 1901.

Littlewood, Arthur (editor): *Indian Mutiny and Beyond: The Letters of Robert Shebbeare VC*, 2007.

London Standard, 28 September 1854.

Lucknow Album, the: held in the British Library. It is a photographic record of prominent residents of Lucknow, both European and Indian, directly before the siege. The album was formerly owned by *The Times* war correspondent William H. Russell, who was presented with it by Captain Trevor Wheler. The bookplate has the inscription: 'Headquarters Camp, Dilkoosha, Lucknow, March 15th 1858. Presented to me by Trevor Wheler (signed) – W. H. Russell.' The album was compiled before the Siege of Lucknow (May 1857) and features the work of a local photographer, Ahmad Ali Khan, from 1856 and early 1857. Many of the prints are annotated by hand, presumably by Wheler and Russell, giving the names of the sitters, and sometimes their fate in the siege.

Lutfullah, Sayed: *Azimullah Khan Yusufzai: The Man Behind the War of Independence, 1857*, 1970.

McIlwraith, Thomas F.: *The Indian Empire: It's History, Topography, Government, Finance, Commerce, and Staple Products: With a Full Account of the Mutiny of the Native Troops*,

MacMunn, Lieutenant-General, Sir George: *The Indian Mutiny in Perspective*, 1931.

Malleson, Colonel George Bruce: *Red Pamphlet*, 1857.

Malleson, Colonel George Bruce: *History of the Indian Mutiny, 1857–58*, (Volumes 3 to 6) 1878–80.

Malleson, Colonel George Bruce: *Ambushes and Surprises*, 1885.

Marshman, John Clark: *Memoirs of Major-General, Sir Henry Havelock CBE*, 1867.

Mason, Philip: *A Matter of Honour: An Account of the India Army, Its Officers and Men*, 1974.

Metcalfe, Private Henry: *The Chronicle of Private Henry Metcalfe, 32nd Regiment*, 1953.

Minet Library, Lambeth Archive Department: Henrietta Thornhill Diaries (orphan of Robert and Mary Thornhill, 1879.

Misra, Amaresh: *War of Civilisations, India AD 1857*, 2007.

Mitchell-Forbes, William: *Reminiscences of the Great Mutiny, 1867–59*, 1893.

Mukherjee, Rudrangshu: *Spectre of Violence.*

Mukherjee, Rudrangshu, *Satan Let Loose Upon Earth: The Kanpur Massacres in India in the Revolt of 1857. Past and Present Magazine*, August 1990.

Munro, Surgeon-General William: *Reminiscences of Military Service with the 93rd Sutherland Highlanders*, 1883.

Murphy, Private: Memorandum of Private Murphy, late of the 84th Regiment, narrating events during the siege of Cawnpore (Khanpur) in 1857 (supporting his application for employment in the Corps of Commissionaires – Wellcome Library, 1869.

Murray, Mrs: *Another Account of the Cawnpore Massacre. The Hobart Town Daily Mercury*, 2 November 1858 and 18 February 1859.

Navy and Army Illustrated: 'The 17th Lancers in the Embers of the Mutiny', 21 February 1896.

National Library of Scotland.

Neill, Colonel James George Smith: Telegrams to Colonel Birch CB, dated 28 June and 5 July 1857.

Nevill DSO, Captain H. L., Royal Artillery: *Campaigns on the North-West Frontier*, 1912.

New Oxford Dictionary of National Biography, The, 2004.

Probett, Mark: *For My Family: Cawnpore in the Year of 1857*, (privately printed).

Raikes, Colonel Thomas: *Services of the 102nd Regiment of Foot (Royal Madras Fusiliers) from 1842 to the present time: Being a sequel to the: 'Services of the Madras European Regiment, by a Staff Officer'*, 1867.

Ramsey, Lt-Colonel Balcarres Dalrymple Wardlaw: *Rough Recollections of Military Service and Society (volume one)*, 1882.

Raven-Hill, Leonard: *Indian Sketch-Book*, 1903.

Rawlins, General J. S.: *The Autobiography of an Old Soldier, 1843–1879* (privately printed).

Reading Central Library.

Robinson, Jane: *Angels of Albion: Women of the Indian Mutiny*, 1996.

Russell, William Howard: *My Indian Mutiny Diary*, 1857.

Ryder, Private John (32nd Regiment): *Four Years Service in India*, 1853.

Saran, Renu: Freedom Struggle of 1857.

Saunders, Lieutenant Frederick John Gothleipe: *Personal Papers held in the Archives of the York and Lancaster Regiment* and in *The National Archives.*

Schawohl, Eva: *The Lucknow Residency*, 2016 and 2018.

Shepherd, William Jonah: *A Personal Narrative of the Outbreak and Massacre at Cawnpore during the Sepoy Revolt of 1857*, 1879.

Shepherd, William Jonah: *Guilty Men of 1857: England's Great Mission to India*, 1879.

Sherer, John Walter: Letter to W. Muir dated 30 August 1857 in Records of the Intelligence Department of the North-West Province of India.

Sherer, John Walter: *Cawnpore Narrative*, 1859.

Sherer, John Walter: *Daily Life During the Indian Mutiny*, 1910.

Sherer, John Walter: *Havelock's March on Cawnpore, 1857: A Civilian's Notes*, 1910.

Smith, Leonard: *A South-Lakeland Nautical Dynasty: Captain Joseph Fayrer of Milnthorpe*, 2012.

Somerset Archive and Record Office: Dodson and Pulman solicitors acting for the will and estate of Isabella Georgina White, 1858 and 1861.

Spectator Archive, the: 11 June 1859.

Streets, Heather: *The Rebellion of 1857: Origins, Consequences and Themes*, 2001.

Swiney, Colonel G. C.: *Historical Records of the 32nd Light Infantry, now the 1st Battalion, Duke of Cornwall's LI, from the Formation of the Regiment in 1702 Down to 1892, compiled and edited by*, 1893.

Sydney Morning Herald, the: 19 October 1857.

Taylor, P. J. O.: *Chronicles of the Mutiny and Other Historical Sketches*, 1992.

Taylor, P. J. O.: *A Star Shall Fall*, 1995.

Telegraph, the Brisbane: 8 September 1900.

Thomson, Captain Mowbray: Letter to *The Times* newspaper dated 8 September 1858.

Thomson, Captain Mowbray: *The Story of Cawnpore*, 1859.

Tickell, Alex: *Cawnpore, Kipling and Charivari: 1857 and the Politics of Commemoration*, October 2009.

Times, the: 29 September 1857, 11 November 1857.

Tope, Parag: *Tatya Tope's Operation Red Lotus*, 2010.

Tracey, Lance-Corporal David, 84th Regiment: Letter to a comrade in Dum Dum, 1857.

Trevelyan, Sir George Otto: *Cawnpore*, 1866.

United Service Gazette, 1858, part II.

Urwick, the Younger, William: *Indian Pictures: drawn with pen and pencil*, 1881.

Vansittart (formerly Jervis), *Mary Amelia: Personal Diaries, 1842–1858*.

Vibart, Colonel Henry Meredith: *Addiscombe: Its Heroes and Men of Note*, 1894.

Vibart, Colonel Edward Daniel Hamilton: *The Sepoy Mutiny as seen by a Subaltern from Delhi to Lucknow*, 1898.

Walsh, Paddy: The Walsh Family and the Cawnpore Massacre. The Journal of the Families in British India Society (FIBIS) number 31, spring 2014.

Walsh, Reverend John Johnston: *A Memorial of the Futtehgurh Mission and her Martyred Missionaries, With Some Remarks on the Mutiny in India*, 1858.

Ward, Andrew: *Our Bones Are Scattered: The Cawnpore Massacres and the Indian Mutiny of 1857*, 1996.

War Office Records held at Kew (many and various).

Waterfield, Private Robert (32nd Regiment): *The Memoirs of Private Robert Waterfield, 1842–1857*, 1968.

Western Mail, Perth, Australia: 17 January 1929.

Western Australian, Perth, Australia: 20 June 1936.

Williams, Colonel George Walter: *Dispositions (On the Mutiny of 1857) Taken at Cawnpore under the Direction of Colonel GWW*, 1858.

Williamson, Donald Creighton: *The York and Lancaster Regiment*, 1968.

Wise MD, James: *The Diary of a Medical Officer during the Great Indian Mutiny of 1857*, 2009.

Wolseley, Garnet: *From England to Cawnpore for the Great Indian Rebellion*, ND.

Wylly, Colonel Harold Carmichael: *The York and Lancaster Regiment, 1758–1919*, 1920.

Yalland, Zoe: *Traders and Nabobs: The British in Cawnpore, 1765–1857*, 1987.

Yalland, Zoe: *Boxwallahs: The British in Cawnpore, 1857–1901*, 1994.

York and Lancaster Regiment Museum, Rotherham.

Index